All Alone?

All Alone?

Help and Hope for Single Parents

by Jill Worth and
Christine Tufnell

First published in 1997 by Hodder and Stoughton Ltd.

This edition published 2001 by Spring Harvest Publishing Division
and Paternoster Lifestyle
07 06 05 04 03 02 01   7 6 5 4 3 2 1

Paternoster Lifestyle is an imprint of Paternoster Publishing,
PO Box 300, Carlisle, Cumbria CA3 0QS, UK
and Paternoster Publishing USA
Box 1047, Waynesboro, GA 30830-2047
www.paternoster-publishing.com

British Library Cataloguing in Publication Data

A catalogue record for this book is available from the British
Library

ISBN 1-85078-439-6

Cover design by Campsie
Printed in Great Britain by
Bell and Bain, Glasgow

Contents

Foreword

Some years ago I was invited to take part in a seminar on relationships in the family. It was the coffee interval, I was the next speaker and I was sitting on the edge of the stage waiting for the session to start. Suddenly a woman approached me; she was about thirty-five years old and had obviously been crying. She sat down next to me and I asked her what was wrong. She explained that the previous speaker had stressed the importance of a father in the life of a child. Turning to me she said, 'My children have no father; he left years ago. Are they destined to be failures?'

I listened for a while as she talked and then said, 'I don't know you, but you sound as though you are a fantastic mother. Don't believe for another second that your children are certain to fail.' I then gave her the details of an organisation that works to help single parents feel they are not alone. It seems she found that brief bit of encouragement was life-changing and she later wrote to tell me the most wonderful news about her children.

These days I never begin one of our seminars without specifically welcoming those who are single parents. I believe they have the hardest job on the face of the earth. They sometimes have a hard time in the media, but what so often doesn't come across is the tenacity, sheer dedication and hope that most single parents have. And, over the years, I have met so many who are not only doing that job of parenting so very well, but who are also inspiring others not to lose heart. Let me mention two.

Stacey lives in Zambia. I met her on a trip I made with Tear Fund. She had lost both her parents to AIDS. When her mother died her relatives wanted to share her six younger brothers and sisters around but the kids wouldn't hear of it. They said that they must stay together. Stacey became a mother too young.

I asked her what was the most difficult thing about her situation. 'Oh,' she said, 'The girls want clothes and the boys want money.' I have heard those same complaints from hundreds of parents but never before when 'clothes' could mean 'two odd shoes for school', and 'money' the few pence a day which might be earned by selling a little paraffin outside the house.

As Stacey spoke with us her arm was around her younger sister Angela, aged fifteen. They were both beautiful, and yet so very vulnerable. I asked Stacey what it was like to be a parent at such an age and if she ever spoiled the youngest – Collins – aged ten. Stacey replied with all the seriousness of one who has learned big lessons fast. 'No – he has to make his own way in life. He works hard at school. He is number one in his class.' We talked about the loneliness of having to do such a task without other adult help. She said, 'I miss my mother and my father; but we can do it. We cannot live in the past – we have to look forward.'

Somebody asked Stacey if she ever thought of marriage. She said, 'Yes – but whoever takes me must take my brothers and sisters as well. I know this will require a special man, but that is what I am praying for. I want a husband, not just a relationship.'

I sat and listened as though I was at the feet of an old woman sharing wisdom gleaned over a hundred years instead of to a young woman barely into adulthood. The moment was too precious to miss. I had to ask her something else. 'Stacey, in the United Kingdom I run seminars for parents – hundreds of people often come to them. If you could pass on one piece of advice what would it be?' Stacey smiled and spoke without hesitation, as if all her life she had known the answer. 'You must be there for your children. If you are not there, any advice you give them doesn't work. There must be love – that way you will feel what your children are feeling.'

'Stacey,' I promised, 'I will tell parents about you for the rest of my life.'

The other single parent who so affected me was somewhat older than Stacey but I have never forgotten the story she shared with me. I was at the back of the auditorium shaking hands with people as they left, when she came up to me. I had been talking about the power of unconditional love and it was obvious that something I had said had touched this woman's heart, but I am in her debt for what she told me that day has never left me.

She was a lone parent and her son was twenty-three years old. She had tried hard to encourage him in the Christian faith and he used to go to church but somebody had offended him and he had stopped attending. She told me that her son was a punk rocker; in fact, he was the most outrageous punk rocker in the whole of her city. His head was shaved apart from a piece in the centre which stood up like the tail of a cockatoo and was bright orange. He wore a ring through his nose and cheek. He dressed in leather gear and wore a little mascara.

The previous week he had been helping her shop in a local supermarket. When they were at the check-out he said, 'I'm going to get some cigarettes then I'll come back and help you pack.' The moment he had left the assistant at the check-out commented, 'How can you bear to be seen out with him when he looks like that?' The lone parent mum said to me, 'I smiled at her and replied, "Oh, my dear, it's very easy. You see I have brought him up through all these years. I love him. *He's my son.*"'

I am thrilled to commend this book to you – whether you are a single parent yourself or whether you are trying to understand the issues that face lone parents every day of their lives. Jill and Christine are special women. They have done it, been there and worn the T-shirt. And their advice has a wonderful blend of realism and *hope*.

I pray this book will be a real help to you in your journey through single parenting. Since Care for the Family first started we have sought to support single parents; these days we have a department dedicated to that task. If ever we can help you in any way don't hesitate to let us know.

Rob Parsons

1

The beginning of the journey

Every lone parent has a unique story. Whether divorced, separated, widowed or never married, all have travelled along their own individual road to bring them to where they are now.

But they have one thing in common. Almost every single parent has become one through crisis. Only a tiny minority actually choose to have and rear a child on their own.

It would have been good to have a fairy tale ending '...and they lived happily ever after'. No one expects to be left, literally holding the baby. They didn't make divorce plans when they said their vows. They didn't expect their partner to be killed in an accident, to be terminally ill or to commit suicide. They didn't plan for their husband to leave them for another woman or their wife to decide she couldn't cope with family life any more. Many thousands are finding out the hard way about single parenting – through their own, private crisis.

Sally thought her marriage had been all right. They had everything – a nice house, a car, enough money to afford a few luxuries. Enough for Sally to leave work and stay at home when their daughter Karen was born. Karen was now three, and she was adorable. Sally accepted Sam's business trips and the late office hours. When she'd challenged him about his secretary he had been angry and accused her of jealousy. Perhaps she had too much time to think. She devoted her energies to being the perfect mother. Sam even encouraged her to spend a week staying with an old school-friend.

Sally caught an earlier train home than expected. She felt uneasy, but couldn't explain it. Unlocking the door quietly, she left Karen playing in the lounge and went upstairs to her bedroom. Clearly she had arrived too soon. The evidence of the previous night's activities was there in front of her. Picking up the unfamiliar packet of condoms, she hurled them at Sam. 'Get out! Get out! Get out!' After a terrible scene, he left. For weeks, the battle raged within her. 'I'll wake up from the nightmare soon; I've no money; I won't be able to cope; I'm a useless mother; I can't go on.'

Paul wandered aimlessly from room to room. He sat down and immediately got up. The silence was deafening. He turned on the radio but quickly switched it off. Everything reinforced what he'd lost. As he closed his eyes, he could see them all there – Val in the kitchen making supper; Peter stretched out on the carpet making a constant noise as he moved his cars into place; Alison always chattering, 'Daddy, listen, at school my friend Claire...' But they weren't there any more. They'd gone to live with Dave.

He'd been friends with Dave since junior school. They'd fought together, played football, taken old motorbikes apart, shared holidays. He'd never have believed Dave could take his wife. Something must have got into her. She would never have done this on her own. How could she just walk out and take Peter and Alison with her? Now he knew how carefully it must have been planned – every detail – even every penny meticulously accounted for. Well, she was in for a surprise! He'd show her. Her staid, boring husband was going to change!

It was quiet now. Everyone had left. The funeral had gone well. A nice service, and so many people there. She was glad it hadn't rained. Tom had been a good husband. He'd always looked after them. He'd been kind and gentle. He used to smile at her, with just a twinkle in his pale blue eyes, when he teased her about her passion for collecting teddy bears. Her eyes filled with tears. She stopped suddenly, taut and tense. She didn't want those more recent memories – the grey, drawn face, the body reduced to skin and bones. She rushed round the house to find all the photographs of the husband she once knew. She mustn't lose that image of him; that image of life.

'Mummy, what are you doing?' Jamie asked. Sarah hugged him tightly. He was all she had left now.

Why? Why? Why had she listened to him? Why had she believed him? Why had she agreed? How could she have been so naïve? Why did this have to happen to her? Jane moved awkwardly. No position was comfortable these days. She looked down at the growing lump. He'd wanted her to have an abortion. 'Get rid of it. No one'll know. Don't let it spoil our relationship. I'm not staying here with a baby around. It's your choice. The baby or me. And that's final.'

Jane had watched him walk away. She'd sat by the phone for days, not daring to go out. Perhaps she should have had the abortion after all? She'd rushed to collect every post, but only bills had dropped on the mat. How could she have been so stupid? And at her age too! No one would want her now, with a baby and no wedding ring.

Andrew collapsed into the old armchair and switched on the television. He would allow himself half an hour, he thought. But after five minutes, he fell asleep. He was just so tired these days. There was so much to do each day. Going to the office was a relief – there he could escape some of the pain of life outside. But even there, although he tried hard to get his mind fixed on the figures on the screen, Bill had to correct his mistakes.

Home meant an endless round of cleaning, cooking, shopping, washing and ironing. The effort of looking after three teenagers was too much for him. Earlier he'd forgotten to take Alec's red jumper out of the pile before pushing the lot into the washing machine. Now everyone was complaining of red clothes. 'Buy yourselves some new ones,' he'd retorted, and mentally added another figure to his overdraft. It was all right for his wife to say he'd cope now the boys were older. She was with Geoff.

Bang! Lynn closed the front door of their flat for the last time. Picking up her battered suitcase and numerous carrier bags in one hand, she pushed the buggy with the other. 'Hold on tight to the handle,' she commanded Sean. It had taken her months to reach this point, and she almost turned back. Resolutely she turned her face towards the end of town and the large rambling house where temporary refuge awaited her. She thought of all the rows. The nights she'd spent in fear of the beatings and the pain. Yet she'd loved him. He was strong, and good-looking in a rugged sort of way. He'd swept her off her feet. They were going to conquer the world together. Nothing had prepared her for the revulsion of rape as he watched pornographic videos. She looked behind her, jumping at the sound of footsteps. Would she ever be free?

Annie stood on the doorstep and watched as her husband drove away. After almost twenty years of a marriage where she had been unloved, belittled and repeatedly betrayed, her main emotion was intense relief. Her friends told her she had been abused for years, but she thought abuse was being physically or sexually attacked. Inside, though, she knew they were right. She had tried everything to make her marriage work but now she knew that if her husband didn't agree to go, she would be in a mental hospital very soon.

Yes, she was relieved, but she ached from the pain of it all. Divorce hadn't been an option so far as she was concerned. And yet she knew that things had become so terrible for her and for the children that this separation had to happen. If I had cancer, she thought, and an operation would save my life, then however much I would rather not have the operation, I would have to go ahead. My marriage was so terrible that it was cancerous, and a separation will save my life. However much I would rather not separate, I have to go ahead. And just like an operation, I will recover. But I will be scarred for life.

She shut the front door and went into the living room, where the children looked up at her with wide eyes. In time she would discover that their main emotion, too, was relief that their father had left. But there was a long way to go – there were so many more painful emotions for them all to deal with first.

He started packing his suitcase. As always, he folded each shirt carefully. What had he said the night before? 'I'm going away for the weekend and I don't know if I'll be coming back.' Suddenly all the pieces of the jigsaw fell into place. The late nights, the unexplained changes in mood, the sense of foreboding. They all pointed to one thing. He had found someone else.

Janet shouted to the boys. 'Get dressed. We'll have breakfast at Grandma's.' She phoned for a taxi. She couldn't stay to watch the man she loved walk out. She gathered up some toys, still strewn over the floor after Christmas. She was in shock; this was all so sudden, so totally unexpected. This can't be true, she thought. But it was true. He never came back. And she was three months pregnant.

All true stories, all crises, and all unique. All first steps on the start of a long journey without a clear route. On the road ahead there are many obstacles to be overcome, mountains to climb and valleys to cross.

The aim of this book is to be a travel companion to parents on that journey, whether they're just starting out or a long way down the roa

Your personal journey may not look so neat! But many single parents experience these stages. You can't go back to the way things were before becoming a single parent, but you can climb up to face the future with more confidence and strength.

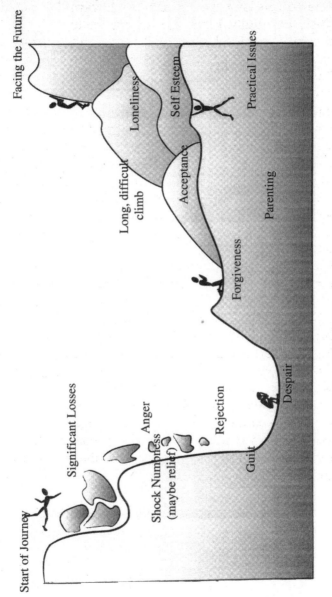

Start of Journey

Significant Losses

Shock Numbness
(maybe relief)

Anger

Rejection

Guilt

Despair

Forgiveness

Long, difficult climb

Acceptance

Loneliness

Self Esteem

Parenting

Practical Issues

Facing the Future

The Single Parent Journey

2

Loss

Anyone who becomes a single parent goes through a bereavement experience. It's not only those who have lost a partner through death who have to go through that valley, but those who have become single parents through separation and divorce. It's been said that divorce is like a death without a funeral. In the loss and pain, many similarities exist between those who have lost their partner through death and those who separate.

But for the separated or divorced single parent, there can also be great differences. Many say they wish their partner had died, rather than left the family. They have to cope with the added pain of the fact that their partner chose to leave; that they were rejected. Or to cope with the fact that they themselves made the decision to end the marriage relationship. And they cannot usually identify with the good memories of the marriage that widows and widowers are often left with.

If a partner has died, the funeral allows for an outward sign of the finality of death and a public opportunity to say goodbye. The pain is intense, and the loss, whether sudden or expected, is great. But the divorced single parent can feel that while the widow or widower receives understanding and sympathy from others, similar support is often sorely lacking for them.

The shock of death is its finality. But for some separated parents, it is the very uncertainty of separation which tears at them. Often in the months following separation, especially if it was sudden, there is the possibility of a return, of reconciliation. It is this hope which can cloud the reality of the present situation. For some, this denial can go on for years. It's possible to live in a false world, believing the partner is going to return. This is a dangerous and unreal place to be in, since the partner who has been left can't move on in life.

However it occurs, becoming a single parent means loss. To be heartbroken by the loss of a partner is an intense physical and emotional experience. Some parents told us of their reactions in the early days. Anne says, 'In the days leading up to the parting, I felt despair. I thought I was dying. I didn't believe anyone could feel so much emotional pain and still be alive. I felt hopeless, helpless, worthless and abandoned.' Mary remembers, 'My feelings were numb. I felt as if I was having a bad dream,' while Elizabeth says, 'I felt relief at first, then emptiness. I was angry and frustrated when the practical difficulties of living with my parents became apparent.' Tom was 'suicidal, sad, confused, and very angry' and John says his feelings were 'absolute stunned shock. I ate little and slept little.'

In the early days, it's quite common to feel numb, to operate on two levels at once. The visible level is robotic, on automatic pilot: feeding the children, loading the washing machine, answering the telephone. The emotional level is like a volcano waiting to erupt. It's possible to operate efficiently, and for others to say, 'Hasn't he taken it well. So brave!'

It's as though the emotions would go into overload, so a fuse has blown to give time for the whole person to recover a little. This condition of shock is the natural way for the body to react and cope with the crisis. To pretend whatever has happened has not in fact happened is a defence mechanism which is helpful, at least for a while. It is not until later that the volcano starts to erupt, sometimes slowly and sometimes with great force. The reality of grief and pain can hit hard.

During the time of numbness, when people are least able to function normally, they are often required to make far-reaching decisions, face new challenges and accept extra responsibilities. It does help to have the support of family and friends. As the practicalities of everyday living are the most urgent, it's necessary to address these first. Often, emotional upheavals have to be left to a later date, when there is more time to face them.

Becoming a single parent starts with the loss of a partner, but many other losses will follow. Loss of a partner can also mean loss of money, home, possessions, family, friends, job. It can mean loss of children, through limited or no contact, and the loss of shared parenting. Loss of identity, confidence and security; of perceived future, status, respect; faith; loss of group identity for couples.

Loss of money
Money, or more often lack of it, can become a major burden. Those who do have a home, and enough income to support their family, can count this as a great blessing in the midst of their suffering. At the very least, it's one less thing to worry about. For most single parents, the loss of a partner means a loss of income, and for many it means serious hardship.

The main breadwinner may have gone, and now there is little income to support the family. Added to the usual expenses of living, there may be a funeral or court case to pay for. Visit the DWP and claim all that you are entitled to. Read DWP leaflets, enlist the help of a friend and use the local Citizens Advice Bureau if there seem to be difficulties.

Maintenance should provide for the children – in theory. But there are hurdles to cross first. The ex-partner must not only be traceable, but must also have some money. Even when the parent with the children is awarded maintenance, this will still almost invariably result in a substantial drop in income. The ex-partner will have their own living expenses, and two households cannot live as economically as one.

This drop in income will affect single parenting. Now the children can't have the clothes, toys or holidays they may have been used to. And neither can you. Just clothing and feeding the children adequately becomes a burden.

It's not only the parent with day-to-day responsibility for the children who will be struggling financially. The absent parent will also be facing sacrifice as they pay maintenance for their children, as well as housing costs in their new home. Practical changes in lifestyle become necessary, and it's not easy to accept less than was possible before.

Financial hardship is often severe. Every bill is dreaded. Learning to budget is essential. Read Chapter 6, **Managing your money**, for some suggestions.

The loss of income is difficult whatever standard of living the family was used to. Janet visited Anne's new home, a detached house in a rural area. As Anne showed her round, Janet admired the decor and the new furniture which all matched and fitted the rooms. To Janet, living with her three children in her parents' small house, this was luxury. But Anne lamented the loss of her previous large house with extensive gardens and swimming pool. Everything is relative, and to Anne her loss seemed just as great as Janet's.

The long-term view may be bleak. While initially it's

possible to manage quite well on a low income, it's the ongoing situation which is hard. Non-stop penny-counting can be dispiriting, and can add to the overall feelings of bitterness and depression. And then the household items begin to wear out and need replacing; children attend a new school and need full uniform; or the water pipe bursts and a plumber is needed.

Working out your own priorities in spending will provide some guidelines. Some single parents will feel that it is right for them to stay at home and manage on the income they receive. Others will decide to continue or seek paid employment. For many it seems they have no choice but to continue work. It's a matter to discuss with trusted friends or family and to think out logically. Money does matter, but it has to be balanced against the whole needs of the family. What is right for one single parent family may be wrong for another.

Here are some points to be considered:

- How much income do I need to provide for myself and my family? Will this cover basics?
- How can I learn to accept a lower standard of living than I previously enjoyed?
- Do I have paid employment now? Can I make suitable arrangements for my children?
- Do I have training, qualifications or experience which will help me get a job?
- What conditions do I want to impose? For example, only work in school terms; work between 9 a.m. and 3 p.m. Monday to Friday; must be within walking distance.
- Will I gain financially? Consider the losses of Income Support, free dental treatment, etc. Can I apply for Working Families Tax Credit?
- What arrangements can I make for the children? What

if one of them is ill? Am I satisfied that the children
will be safe and well cared for?

● Would the children benefit from the extra material
gains?

● Would the children benefit from my involvement
with the working world? Would I be more stimulated
by my job and less dependent on my children for contact outside home?

● Will possible financial security affect possible emotional insecurity caused by my long hours at work?

● Can I physically cope with parenting by myself and a
job?

If we can make considered decisions then we can feel
more at peace about them, and we don't need to feel
guilty about the negative effects of either paid employment or staying at home. Either decision will have
advantages and disadvantages. We need to weigh them
and then decide. Circumstances may seem to dictate the
answer to us, but as they change we may need to consider the subject again.

Some parents who were going out to work before the
break-up of their marriage may feel it right to give up
their job. It may give them time to recover physically
and emotionally from the trauma, and the children may
benefit from their presence. It would also make the more
practical aspects of child care easier. However, it will
mean another loss, and that should be recognised. The
loss of a job will mean loss of status, loss of outside interest and companionship, loss of a perhaps fulfilling job
which may serve to take your mind off things for a few
hours each day. Some newly-single parents view their
job as a lifeline, and to give it up would be the final
straw.

Loss of home

Losing a home may be unavoidable. Sometimes the rent or mortgage arrears are so great that moving is inevitable. Others have tied accommodation, for example clergy, police, army or residential care workers. For others, their partner may have so ill-treated them that the only way to safety is to leave. Refuges for battered wives are nationwide, and usually full to overflowing. The relief from abuse will be tinged with the loss of the familiar home. Low-cost housing and council housing is not easily obtained.

Moving home adds to the already existing trauma for you and for your children. It is helpful to look at any advantages the move affords, and not to be surprised at the emotional toll it may take.

For those who have a choice in whether to move, taking time to consider all the aspects will help you to make a healthier decision. To some people, the idea of moving house seems like the panacea for removing past hurtful memories. They may think, 'This was the house where my husband brought another woman while I was away; where my children were abused; where my wife died; this is the room in which she told me she was leaving.' A new house, breaking unhelpful ties with the past, seems to equal a new life. It may seem like that – but remember, you take yourself with you. It may mean just escaping from the hurt without dealing with it. Some people advise those who have recently been bereaved never to move within the first few months, if they can avoid it. It can be too easy to make a wrong decision in those first traumatic weeks.

If you do decide to move, it's possible that a new home can give opportunity for a fresh approach to home-making. You can stamp your own character on it, and start again positively. But before you start the ball rolling, look again at the home you have. Can you continue to live in it, despite everything? Is it time to remove the 'presence' of the absent partner: clothes, personal effects? Is it possible to redecorate, move the furniture around or even knock two rooms into one? By experimenting with the home you have you can change the look of it completely; it can be fun and could be a step forward on your single parenting journey.

Loss of possessions

Loss of possessions may seem insignificant compared to loss of money, job or home, but it can still hurt. After a burglary, the victim often laments most the items that have sentimental value. In a divorce settlement the loss of possessions can cause similar pain. Deciding which partner is keeping the treasured antique clock is bad enough; even worse is deciding who is keeping the albums full of photographs of the children growing up. Although these losses are in a sense material, they come on top of the loss of a unique relationship. Focusing on what you do have can take away the pain a little, but it still has to be grieved for and dealt with.

Loss of children

For those single parents who no longer live with their children, and particularly for those who have little or no contact, life can seem a living death.

You've lost the day-to-day care and control, you miss them desperately, you are worried about how they are being brought up, about the influence of the 'other man/woman' your ex may now be with, and about the future relationship you'll have with them. If you do have contact, the relationship may be strained. And it's a terrible wrench each time you have to say goodbye.

Even if your children still live with you but have contact with their other parent, there is an element of loss. You 'lose' them each time they see your ex. And often it's not just for the time they're away, but after they come back. You'd built up a secure relationship with them, and each time they come back it's as if you have to start building all over again. They're not quite 'your' children – and yet you carry most, if not all, the responsibility.

Loss of family relationships
Changes in the family structure also mean changes in family relationships. The death of a husband or wife is to the extended family the death of a son or daughter, brother or sister, uncle or aunt. The relationships with grieving in-laws may be more strained than they once were. The common bond has gone. Most of the previous contact was with, through or because of, the common person. It may need sensitivity on everyone's part to accept the shared pain and grief, and build new bridges.

Grandparents often have a very special relationship with their grandchildren, and there can be two-way comfort between them as they grieve for the person who has died. It is worth the effort required to give the children a good link with this part of their family.

Divorce often means divorce from the partner's family too. Loyalties may be divided and emotions mixed. 'My in-laws always treated me like a son,' said Chris. 'After my own parents' death, they were the only family I had. Now I've lost them as well as my wife.' Often it means children lose contact with this side of the family too. But contact with their grandparents on both sides should be encouraged, and visiting grandparents could be a valuable part of the time spent with the absent parent.

Sometimes the single parent's own family are divided in their reaction. 'Because I was the one to leave the matrimonial home, my brother won't speak to me – he says I've disgraced the family name,' said one mother. 'But my sister was wonderful. She took us on holiday with her. And I don't know what I'd have done without my parents.'

Parents do not cease to be parents when their child marries, or when their child becomes a parent themselves. When death, unplanned pregnancy, separation or divorce occurs, it also affects the parents of the couple, as well as members of the wider family. In the pain of the moment, things may be said or done which are later regretted. Some single parents have felt that their own parents have treated them like children again. Much of this stems from the desire to protect their offspring from further pain. In the early days after the crisis, such mothering can be much appreciated. It is comforting to have others care for and about you. But the time comes when over-mothering should cease. Do not lose sight of the fact that you are an adult, with adult responsibilities of your own.

Loss of friends

You had friends together, as a couple. Now, some have decided that they are taking sides. They find it difficult to stay close to you both, so they choose to keep one partner at arm's length. It's easier for them that way. Others will reject both of you, unable to cope with the traumas you are going through, and unwilling to provide a shoulder to cry on, with all the time and effort that entails. It's at this time that you find out who your true friends are. You're probably better off without the other sort.

Annie discovered that one couple who had helped her and her ex-husband for years, trying to keep them together and help them resolve their marriage problems, dropped them completely once the decision was taken to separate. 'I had been relying on them to help me through – and to help the children through, as well,' she said. 'I don't know whether they felt let down because we'd separated despite their years of befriending us, but whatever it was that made them drop us, they could at least have stuck by the children. The person who helped me through those early years was a woman at my church who I hardly knew before my separation. She took me under her wing and has mothered me ever since.'

Loss of choice

Your life seems to be dictated by others. It wasn't your choice for your partner to leave or to die; it's not your choice that others stepped in to decide things for you – the courts, solicitors, the DWP, perhaps social workers. Decisions about finance and even about your own children seem to be made by others.

This loss is often overlooked, but is very real, and one of the most difficult to come to terms with. People tend to panic or become depressed when they feel out of control. Yet you still have choices that only you can make, as defined at the end of this chapter.

Loss of hope; loss of reason for living

For some people, children, family, wife, husband are their reasons for living. Their family is the reason they go to work, to earn the money to keep them secure together. When the family is blown apart, where do they find their hope?

This loss particularly affects those with older children, or whose children are not with them. The plans for the future, the expectation of celebrating one wedding anniversary after another, welcoming grandchildren to their home together, have all disappeared.

Hazel became a single parent when her husband

retired at sixty-five. He announced he was leaving her for his secretary, after forty years of marriage. All the plans for their retirement home, the years of growing old together, had to be shelved. She had to find a new reason to carry on.

Loss of faith

For Christians, there is an extra dimension to all this – a faith which can help them through, or which can add even more confusion. 'Why did God let my wife die?' 'Why doesn't he bring my husband back?' You may be living alone, while your children are living with your ex-wife or husband, and you're mourning their loss. 'Why has this happened? I didn't want it to.' You may look at your children and see them badly affected by what has happened. How can we trust a God who allows this?

It comes back to that age-old question, why does God allow suffering? Many books have been written on this subject, which only goes to show how hard it is to understand. Anyone hoping that this book will provide an answer to the question will be sorely disappointed. There aren't any glib answers. Sometimes it's only possible to accept by faith what can't be accepted by reasoning. Not a blind faith, but a trust in God who is so much greater and wiser than the human mind can fathom.

All of us will die, and nobody knows why some people die earlier or more painfully than others. Nobody can say why.

When a husband or wife leaves, some newly-single parents will pray for them to return. It's natural to ask for God to make it all right again. But everyone has been given free will. No one is a puppet, having to do what God wants. Our partners are no exception to that rule. If they decide not to return, they have the freedom to make that choice.

When your world has collapsed, it can sometimes be a struggle to hang on to God at all. There are times when you may cry out to him in anger, and other times when you feel peaceful and secure in his love. He understands both states of mind and all the emotions in between. On your emotional rollercoaster, you may change on an hourly basis but God never changes.

Loss of the marriage/couple relationship

Amid all this loss and bereavement, the most obvious loss of all is the loss of the partner. That loss will be unique to you. All the positive and negative attributes of that person will be missed – some perhaps with relief, others with a desperately sad grief. You've lost not only your partner, but a parent for your child. For some, the loss of a partner will mean the loss of a best friend. For all, the loss of a unique relationship will affect your innermost being, causing you for a time to lose something of yourself, too.

The intimate relationship and sexual bonding between a man and a woman is far stronger than society today usually acknowledges. In marriage, two people are not just linked together like a seam, but fused together like wire, to become a new interwoven whole. Breaking that trust does not simply divide the seam, it destroys the whole. The phrase 'torn apart' expresses the pain of the loss of the state of marriage.

The married state you were known by in society and among family and friends has gone, and it is impossible to revert to your previous position before you were married. Your status has changed. Some women still prefer to be known as Mrs but that very title, in the world's eyes, means that you should have a Mr waiting for you at home. And you haven't.

The time has come to face hard facts. It may not be your chosen position to be a single parent, but it is your actual state. It has happened. You are a single parent. To deny this is being false to yourself.

Each person has a choice. They can choose to be crushed, or choose to build on what they have been through. They can choose to wallow where they are, or to start on the steps towards healing and wholeness. They are not easy steps, but choosing to take them means lives can be rebuilt. It will take honesty and courage. Honesty with yourself, as you accept your situation, is a good start. Being honest with others will allow them to help where possible, practically, emotionally and spiritually.

Sadly, the description 'single parent' carries with it a stigma in society today. For 'single parent', read 'problem'! The media doesn't help the single parent's self-worth. Nor do many politicians. But while you can't change other people's attitudes overnight, you can evaluate and change yours. Forget what the media might say. The term 'single parent' does not have to incorporate ideas of immorality, inferiority or scrounging. The term is simply a description of the fact that for whatever reason the two natural parents of the child are not raising the child together. So hold your head up high!

Sue's story

Sue and her husband Joe were married in 1969. Joe was self-employed; his father had retired, and he part owned, part rented the family farm.

That summer, Joe injured his back while hay-making. Throughout their twenty years of marriage, hospital and doctors' visits were regular, but Joe refused to rest. In January 1989 he had an operation to remove the damaged discs in his back. The operation went wrong, and he was left paralysed from the waist down. He was removed to a spinal injuries unit and had to use a wheelchair.

'It was a time of great trauma and depression,' says Sue. 'I determined to give all the support, care and attention I could to my husband and the business.

'Joe hated his time in hospital, refused counselling and taught himself to walk again. He came back home to manage the farm, but seemed changed towards us. His life had been shattered, and we were estranged. He sued the hospital, and sought the friendship of a neighbour who was unhappy in her marriage. This eventually turned into an affair.

'We all struggled on, but he wanted to be by himself. As the atmosphere at home was so unhealthy for the children, I helped arrange this. I took them to live in a separate house in a near-by village and was no longer active in the business.'

Sue didn't want to make any other major changes for the sake of the children, who were eighteen, fifteen and twelve years old at the time of the separation. She explained to them that their father was ill, very unhappy and wished to live by himself; that he no longer felt he had anything in common with her, and that she was very upset about this. The children were greatly affected by their father's unhappiness, and didn't understand why he wanted to live apart from them.

For a while, Joe became abusive and Sue felt afraid of him. But with the support of her family and friends, she tried to continue life as much like before as possible. Joe was made

*welcome in her new home and had free access to his children.
Before long, Sue and Joe began to be on good terms. For the
first two years after the separation, Sue's aim was to work
towards a reconciliation.*

In the early days, Sue felt great sadness and uncertainty
about the future. She felt betrayed but was determined to survive, and tried to keep busy all the time. She was helped by
being open about her feelings, and by talking at length and in
detail to a wide range of people. Long-term friends helped the
family in practical ways and supported them with telephone
calls and visits. Friends from the church offered help, encouragement and prayer.

Not everyone was so supportive. Some people found the situation difficult to accept, and either condemned Joe or questioned Sue's attitudes. Others even told her where they had
seen Joe and his girlfriend.

Sue found that her Christian faith was a lifeline. She was
not only able to pray about her situation, but could also talk to
and receive counsel from other Christians. She gradually came
to believe that she was going through the suffering for a
reason, and that she should use her experience to help other
people.

The children are all adults now, but Sue says they still need
a solid, dependable base and a supportive parent. After leaving
university, her eldest daughter became unsettled and very
cynical about marriage but Sue points out that she may have
been like that anyway.

There have been no formal access arrangements, but Joe
lives near and the children all visit whenever they want to.
'They've grown to accept the situation,' says Sue. 'They have
low expectations, since they know their father is usually either
out or busy with farm work.'

Looking back, she wishes she had encouraged her husband
to talk earlier about his problems, taken a greater interest in
the business and spent more time with him.

3

Emotions

Submerged, and sometimes crushed, under the sea of loss lies the single parent's sense of identity. Down there too lie the wrecks of their self-esteem, confidence and sense of security. And intertwined with these, tumbling over each other, is a whole mass of emotions.

When the shock and numbness have worn off a little; when the practical details are not quite so urgent as they were at first; when the emotions at last begin to surface – what then?

It's not surprising, having been through a crisis, to have a very strong emotional reaction. It can be so powerful that it dominates and controls the individual. The emotions can be so intense and confused that the whole person feels they are losing control. They need to be separated and examined, in order to be understood.

So what are these emotions? Anger, bitterness, despair, jealousy and revenge are likely to be mixed up with guilt, fear and rejection.

Anger
It's part of human nature to strive for the basic needs of love, security and purpose to be met. Losing partner,

home or children threatens the very foundations of existence. Barbara felt angry because her life, and her children's lives, seemed to be at the mercy of other people's decisions. Her feelings were at the mercy of her husband's actions; her income was at the mercy of the DWP; her children's well-being was at the mercy of the courts; her future home was at the mercy of the Housing Department; her prayers were at the mercy of God.

When Paul's wife, Val, left him to live with his best friend, she took their two children with her. During the following months, Val demanded large sums of money for maintenance. Finally, Paul had to sell the house to give Val half the proceeds. Val rarely allowed him to have the children. Paul was angry. Attacking Val through solicitors only worsened the situation. Bottling up his feelings made him ill and depressed.

Margaret had been married to Harry for eight years. They had been comfortably off, and had been overjoyed when their son and daughter were born. Everything had worked out for them, and they felt as though they were the perfect family. When the hospital phoned to say Harry had been admitted, seriously ill, Margaret was distraught. Her family and friends rallied round. When Harry died, only days later, Margaret screamed at the hospital staff, 'Why did you let him die? Why couldn't you have saved him?'

There are many reasons for anger. You might be angry with:

● Your ex-partner. You may have been treated badly, or you may be terribly jealous of your ex's new relationship. If you were single and became pregnant by a man who immediately ran away from the situation, you may be angry because he did not keep all the promises he made to you. You may even be angry

with your husband or wife because they have died –
particularly if they took their own life.

● Yourself. You may be saying to yourself, 'It's my own
fault I'm in this situation.' Or you can be angry that
you have failed to see what others so clearly saw.

● Other people. They may have let you down; their
actions or words may have caused you pain, and you
may feel they are accusing and blaming you.

● God. Why did he let this happen? He could have
stopped it if he'd chosen to, couldn't he?

The intensity of the anger can be frightening, says single
father Edward. 'The male is the primeval guardian of
"his mate", "his family". The intensity of the anger and
jealousy often leads to thoughts (and sometimes acts) of
violence. And in the process of divorce, men can feel
incensed by the innate unfairness of the legal system
that they think is weighted against them. Men of my
generation (Edward is in his fifties) perceive success in
terms of position in the working situation: wife, children, home are seen as symbols of his success. When put
at risk by another male, together with the possibility of
a substantial loss of income through maintenance, the
reaction is likely to be traumatic. The driver in the situation is the male pride, and the self-esteem which flows
from it.'

It's real to be angry, and it's normal – for a while. It is
not anger that is the problem, it's what you do with it.
Consuming anger is understandable and sometimes jus-
tifiable. But it's also very destructive. You can feed your
anger, remaining furiously angry with everyone and
everything, but in the end it will turn you into a bitter,
cynical and frustrated person. Or you can be honest,
admit you're angry, get your anger out by talking at
length with a trusted friend or counsellor, then look

together at what you can do with it. If it is expressed, it is being defined, and can then be examined.

To deny there is anger merely pushes it further within, sowing the seeds of depression. To be resigned to unjust treatment is to pretend that there is no anger. Letter-writing – a furious letter to your ex, perhaps – can be a means whereby feelings are put into words. Next morning the letter can be torn up or burnt as a symbol of removing the anger. Physical work in the garden or house safely lets out some of the energy of the anger. But it's only too easy to take it out on the children, so if you feel you are stuck in your anger, get help.

Bitterness

Close on the heels of anger follow self-pity and bitterness. 'All I see around me are happy couples with their children.' 'No one understands what it's like for me.' Self-pity is the entrance to the slippery slope of bitterness. Attacks of self-pity are common to everyone, but either they can be warded off or they can hit home and continue their destructive course.

Mary sat alone in her tiny flat with its shared front door. She could hear the neighbours living out their lives through the thin walls. She pictured her husband in his new detached house. When they'd been married, they'd never moved from this place. Now he lived with his second wife, and nothing was denied her. Mary thought, 'I gave him twenty years of my life. I stood by him when he got in trouble with the police. Now I'm here, with nothing and no one. I am absolutely, totally empty. What's the point of living?'

As usual, Jim woke in the early hours, alone in his bed. His thoughts circled in the same way as they did every night. 'I have to manage my job and three kids, and I'm exhausted. I'm not cut out for housework and cooking. I can't go out, and my friends don't call any more. If Anna were still alive, it would be different.'

As these waves of despair relentlessly crash in, you can be engulfed by such sorrow that you feel you're drowning, and if you feel you've sunk so far that you need expert help to reach dry land, there's nothing to be ashamed of in seeking professional assistance. At other times you can emerge, gasping for air. It seems that no one cares or understands the depths of your suffering. The whole world appears to have abandoned you. It is one of life's loneliest experiences.

Janet was helped when she found that even in the worst moments it was possible to find something to be thankful for. When her young son asked her, 'If Daddy loved us, he wouldn't have left, would he?' she wasn't able to answer. She'd endured two months of single parenthood, engulfed in darkness, and at her son's words she broke down. Once she started crying she couldn't seem to stop. Her friend, sitting with her, also in tears, suggested at last that there must be something to be thankful for.

Through her tears, Janet started to count. The boys were healthy and coping with their crisis, with her help. The baby was still safe inside her. With a tremendous effort, she managed to list eight things for which she could be thankful. She started to look up, and never felt quite so low again.

If bitterness remains unresolved, it can eventually destroy. It often needs an act of healing and forgiveness to take place. There will be more on this in the next chapter.

Guilt

'I feel so guilty. I had an affair with another woman, left my wife and children with hardly any warning, and took money from my employers.' Not everyone is able to list their sources of guilt so clearly, but the feelings of guilt, even when undefined, can be just as strong.

Very often the guilt will take the form of 'If only.' 'If only I had made him go to the doctor the minute he found the lump, if only I had another chance, if only I'd been a better wife.' People can get stuck on the treadmill of going back over the past, wishing desperately that it had been different. With hindsight, there will always be some things they could have done differently, or should not have said. Unfortunately it's only easy to rationalise the situation once there has been time to work it out.

But none of this alters the present reality. The clock can't be put back.

There are two kinds of guilt, and only one is real. If you know you have real reason to feel guilty, then don't try to hide it through self-justification, or trying to rationalise your actions. You need to come to terms with what you've done and to accept responsibility, and to do this you need at least a close friend, and in some cases, a counsellor. You need to know that forgiveness is possible, even if restitution is not. But there's a difference between repentance and remorse. Remorse is full of guilt, but it's a hopeless guilt which brings no cure for the pain. Feeling remorseful doesn't mean you hate what you did, but that you feel sorry for yourself because of what you did. But true repentance contains no guilt, and brings healing.

The other sort of guilt is inappropriate. If you're telling yourself you are so bad and it's all your fault, then stop for a minute and ask yourself what specific things you are guilty of. If any, then ask yourself honestly if these things, of themselves, would have made any lasting difference.

It is possible to take on oneself the guilt given by others. Take the scenario of the unfaithful husband, for example. He will fling insults at his astonished wife as he leaves her for another woman. He may tell her she's frigid, she's always nagged, she's never supported him. Such accusations can often be excuses. When the man knows he's at fault – if he's leaving his wife because he's 'in love' with another woman – he has to find reasons to blame his wife for the fact that he's leaving her. It makes him feel less guilty about his own actions.

Then there's the guilt that other people make her feel. The well-meaning friends and relatives who suggest that if she hadn't had a demanding job, and had been at home more, her husband wouldn't have become unhappy. Or that often quoted and damaging excuse that if she'd satisfied him in bed, he wouldn't have had eyes for anyone else. Talk about taking the guilt from the unfaithful husband and putting it squarely, and unfairly, on the shoulders of the wife!

If you're the one who walked out, it's easy to accept the guilt on your own shoulders. Other people will often see you as the guilty partner; after all, it was you who left the marriage, wasn't it? What they don't know is why you left. Only you know whether you bear true guilt or not. You may have left because you couldn't stand being abused any more, or seeing your partner have one affair after another, or seeing your children becoming dreadfully hurt. Again, you have to decide whether the guilt is yours, or whether it's inappropriate.

After Beverly found her husband had been having a series of affairs and wasn't intending to stop, she started divorce proceedings. She carried the guilt for a long time. Her husband hadn't wanted a divorce, and she had. Therefore, she reasoned, she was guilty of ending her marriage. But when a friend finally asked her, 'Who actually broke the marriage vows?' she had to admit it was her husband. 'Then all you did in going for a divorce was to carry that through,' said her friend. 'The marriage had been over for a long time. All you did was ask for a piece of paper to confirm it.'

It's important, perhaps with the help of a friend, to sort out the real guilt from the false. It isn't right to sink beneath a deluge of guilt. Admit to that which is real and true and shed that which isn't.

Fear
Fear can be crippling, emotionally, socially and spiritually. The experience of becoming a single parent can lead to fear of:

- The opposite sex. If you've felt rejected, you may be afraid that if you become involved with anyone else, they too will leave you. Or it may be fear mixed with hatred, believing 'all men will try to control and dominate me like my husband did' or 'all women are fickle and untrustworthy like my wife.' Lynn was afraid of a possible future marriage, particularly the sexual relationship. 'I'd been raped by my ex-husband as he watched pornographic videos. He told me I was fat and ugly. Now I'm afraid I won't be able to respond lovingly to anyone else.'
- Responsibilities. You may feel unable to cope with your children on your own, or frightened of getting into debt.
- Losing the children. It may be that you face custody going to your ex-partner, or that you're afraid your children will themselves opt to go to their other parent. Will they choose to lose contact with you?
- The future. 'What if something happens to me? Who will look after the children?' 'Will my children be taken away?' 'Am I going to die a lonely old woman?'

● Isolation. Joanne was afraid of 'this isolated feeling which descends on me, sometimes becoming a permanent fixture. Even my young son will leave me eventually.' For many single parents without family living near and without supportive friends, isolation is a reality. They are afraid of being ill or succumbing to depression, because the children would have no one to look after them. Also, many people fear being alone in the house, especially at night. Jackie has terrible nightmares and wakes up sweating and terrified. She can't go for comfort to her children, nor does she feel she can phone anyone at 3 a.m. So she sits up in bed with the light on for the rest of the night, waiting for morning and wishing she still had a partner she could cling to.

There are seemingly endless things to fear. It may be that you're afraid of your ex-partner's temper or violence, or of what other people think of you, or that your children will be permanently damaged.

Examine your fear, with a friend if possible. How likely is it that the feared event is actually going to happen? For example, if you're afraid of losing your child to your ex-partner, you might ask yourself: are there any grounds for someone to prove I ill-treat the children? Are they properly fed, clothed and cared for? Do they usually get to school each day? If they are ill, do I take them to the doctor, give them medicine, nurse them? What do the children want? Who do they want to live with?

Sometimes it's possible to take practical steps to reduce the fear. For example, if you're afraid of being taken seriously ill in the middle of the night and having no one to look after the children, ask a trusted friend or family member if you may call on them in an emergency.

Tell the children what the arrangements are. Teach them as early as possible how to summon help. Such crises rarely happen, but if you make plans like this, it can allay your fears.

Fear is part of life, and healthy fear is life-saving (such as a fear of running across a busy road). But if fear dominates and inhibits your daily life, then seek further help.

Rejection

Your previous experience will affect your way of coping and of dealing with all your emotions. This is especially true of rejection. If you feel you have been rejected by your partner, you can have pain almost beyond description. It rocks your self-worth, your security, your desire to be needed. The person who has rejected you has, by actions and words, said, 'You are no good. I don't want you. I don't need you. I'm not here for you in any way. There is nothing you can do to change things.'

Adam was unwanted by his parents. He was told he was ugly. At an early age he was put into care. He can't remember how many homes he lived in. His treatment in those homes wasn't always good. At sixteen he left to fend for himself. At twenty-four he was married. When he was thirty-four, his wife left to live with his best friend. Rejection overwhelmed him.

Clare comes from a loving, caring family. She still feels close to and supported by her parents and siblings. She did well at school and has many friends. When her husband walked out she was deeply hurt. For a while, she was disorientated. But life had taught her that although one man had treated her badly, not everyone was the same. Not everyone felt the same way about her as he did. It will be easier for Clare than for Adam to work through the devastating effects of rejection by their partners.

It's normal to resolve never to be so hurt again, and to build up some form of barrier to protect yourself. You may literally retreat into your own home and avoid people as much as possible. One single mum just watched TV all day, every day. Others may appear to have coped well with their feelings of rejection on the surface, but still don't allow people emotionally close. Still others are so desperate to prove they are lovable that they smother everyone they meet – and it's other people who retreat in self-defence! Some send out such bad messages about themselves that people do reject them, thus proving to themselves that they are right when they say 'nobody loves me'. When Janet was first left alone with her children, she vowed she'd never completely trust another man again. When someone was kind to her, she cried. She felt she didn't deserve it. Now remarried, she says it's a good thing she doesn't feel those things now, or she'd have a very difficult second marriage!

Hiding in your shell or building a strong wall around yourself is only helpful in the short term, while you look for other ways of coping. It covers up the pain, instead of dealing with it. Long-term feelings of rejection need healing. You will need faithful support and care from others to reassure you that rejection is not all your fault. Discovering that others don't treat you the same way as your ex did will give you hope, and help you regain your self-esteem. But although you may know logically that not everyone hates you, it can be difficult for you to realise this deep inside. There are helpful books on the market, and if the roots of your rejection go very deep, counselling can help too. It will take time to rebuild your own self-worth and trust in others.

The whole mass of these intense and overpowering emotions doesn't have to come rushing to the surface all at once. It's better to deal with them like peeling the layers off an onion, separating and removing one at a time. And as with onion-peeling, facing your emotions is accompanied by stinging tears. You may think you're over it, you've cried your last tear – and then a huge surge of emotion overwhelms you. Don't try to stem the tide. If you have someone who'll listen to you, then talk, talk and talk some more. It's vital that feelings are identified, acknowledged and faced honestly, so they can be dealt with. Then deep healing is possible.

Leigh's story

Leigh was devastated when his wife left him, taking their three children, aged thirteen, nine and four.

'I felt utter despair,' he says. 'I lost three stone in weight, going down to seven and a half stone. My work was affected. I had to take a downgrading in job, which meant I also earned less money.

'I didn't want to live, just to fade away. I took on all the guilt of the situation. (It wasn't until years later that I was able to forgive myself.) And I felt very angry towards the man my wife had gone to live with. That gradually lessened, although I found it difficult to be in his presence for some years.'

Friends stepped in to help Leigh practically – with shopping and meals, when he felt he couldn't cope – and to keep him occupied. They allowed him to talk, helping him to understand what was happening. But he found other people – including his mother – less helpful, as they suggested that his wife had been totally responsible for what had happened.

Looking back, Leigh says he wishes he had not been oblivious to potential problem areas, and had been less self-centred. 'I was not as aware of others as I should have been, and did not communicate as I should have done,' he says.

He found it very hard to accept that his children were living apart from him. But he says, 'I realised it was better for them to go with their mum than to stay with their dad, who was in a real state at that time.'

It affected the children badly when they were taken away from the family home. 'I tried to maintain regular visits, and every other weekend the children came to stay with me. It was so difficult for us all to say goodbye at the end of the weekend. And then the family moved much further away, and the interval was extended to every three or four weeks.'

The distance that his children live from him, and the fact that he feels this means he is not being an effective parent is the main ongoing problem Leigh faces now. He makes every effort to see them as often as he can, and to help them whenever he can.

'I've tried to tell them exactly what was happening, and to reassure them, each step of the way,' says Leigh. 'We are all helped, during my contact time, by their love for me, and my total availability and love for them.'

Loneliness isn't as much of a problem as it used to be. It used to strike when Leigh didn't have anything to occupy his mind, or when something reminded him that he was not part of what he calls a 'complete' family. He felt a sense of great sadness and lack of self-worth, as if he was in a dense fog and there was no way out. At those times, he would contact a friend, and try to arrange a walk or lunch together, particularly on Sundays.

Leigh became a Christian after his marriage had broken up. 'It helped me to cope better, and after that, to help others,' he says. 'I have been forgiven, and I have so many wonderful friends.'

4

Forgiveness

It can be incredibly hard to forgive. When there has been deep hurt caused by the loss and/or betrayal of a partner, the act of forgiveness is not the most natural step to take. And when you think your children may have been damaged for life, it may seem impossible to forgive.

Anyway, why should you forgive? You've been so seriously hurt, and you're not going to let your ex off the hook by forgiving them. After all, it's not going to do you any good, is it?

Actually, it is. It's helpful to see forgiveness as letting go, releasing. It doesn't mean pretending the wrong didn't matter, or wasn't really that important. Injustice is wrong and painful, and the wrong remains – whether you forgive or not. But it doesn't have to rule you.

It isn't only the other person you're releasing – it's yourself. You are the one who will suffer if you don't forgive. While you hang on to anger and unforgiveness, you are bound to the other person. You are not free to move on.

To forgive is to give up the right to revenge. Which would you rather do, free yourself to get on with your own life, or go over and over all the wrongs done to you, keep being dominated by getting your own back, fantasising constantly about slashing the wheels on your ex's car or making anonymous phone calls to his new partner?

Giving up that right to revenge doesn't necessarily mean you have to start trusting the other person. Some people think that once they've forgiven their ex, it means they should get back together again. This isn't the case. If the person who has so badly hurt you is not sorry, then it's not possible to have a reconciliation anyway. In time, Janet forgave her husband for leaving her for someone else, but still she doesn't trust him. He continued to lie repeatedly, and after a few years showed he hadn't changed by leaving his second wife in similar circumstances. By forgiving him, Janet was able to let her husband go and to continue her life without bitterness, but she didn't have to enter into any trusting relationship with him.

Sometimes it's hardest of all to forgive ourselves. We have to learn to release ourselves from our self-imposed judgment. Even if we have something to regret, either we can let the failure crush us or we can choose to learn from it. We are sometimes harder on ourselves than we would be on other people.

There is a time for everything on the single parent journey, and the time for forgiveness is not at the very beginning of the road. It's no use well-meaning friends saying, the minute your wife has walked out, 'You must forgive her.' You don't even understand the concept of forgiveness at that stage – you're too numb, too shocked.

A little further along the road, you might feel furious if anyone says you should forgive. How dare they suggest such a thing when you've been so hurt, and when none of it was even your fault! And the suggestion can even add to your guilt, as your thoughts are more along the lines of, 'When I see her next I'll wring her ****** neck!'

The most immediate human reaction is, 'I'll never forgive her.' It's a natural and real emotion, and it will take some time before the whole business of forgiveness can begin. Trying to push someone further along the road than the place they have reached simply doesn't work.

Forgiveness isn't usually possible until the other emotions – anger, guilt, bitterness – have been dealt with. Then the way is open to choose to forgive your partner, other people who have hurt you and – most difficult of all – yourself.

So how is it possible to forgive? Christians, who believe that God has forgiven them, have the example from the Lord's Prayer, 'Forgive us our sins, as we forgive those who have sinned against us.' If they have received forgiveness, they shouldn't refuse to forgive others. There is the example of Jesus on the cross, crying from the depths of physical, emotional and spiritual pain, 'Father, forgive them...' But how is it even remotely possible to follow that example?

You may not feel like forgiving. But it is possible to 'will' the desire to forgive. Janet's minister, David, put it like this:

First, you say it. Speaking it out loud makes it legal and shows that you wish to be able to forgive.

Second, you mean it. You are engaging your will; you really do want to forgive.

Third, you feel it. That is an emotional stage where something changes inside you and you are no longer being held back by an invisible but strong tie.

Finally, you forget the wrong that has been done to you. 'Forget – how can I?' you may ask. Well, the Hebrew word for 'forget' can mean 'to wither' or 'to cease to care'. In time, instead of having to remember to forget, you will find yourself forgetting to remember. You will then be free to walk forward into the future, released from the past and no longer a victim.

How long will all this take? Steve Hebden, in his book *Rejection*, says, 'Forgiveness may need to be a process. You may need to keep forgiving until the pain goes. How long is that? Until the pain goes.'

Wendy's first marriage ended twenty years ago. Her husband, Andrew, had left her and their two sons. Ten years later, Wendy married again, but her second husband died two years afterwards. She worked through many difficult and painful times, and came through with a quiet but firm faith. One morning the telephone rang. She didn't immediately recognise Andrew's voice. They had lost touch over the years, and she didn't even know where he lived.

Andrew said he was ringing to ask her to forgive him. 'I'm sorry for all I've done,' he said. 'I blamed you for everything. It wasn't true. I said you were a bad wife, that you wouldn't let me see the kids, when in reality it was me who chose not to see them. Now I've given my life again to God. Please will you forgive me?' Wendy was able to tell him that she had forgiven him many years ago, but only now was he able to receive it.

Annie found it hard to forgive her ex for the years of pain he had inflicted on her, but much, much more difficult to forgive him for the pain he had caused the children. One day, two years after her separation, her friend called round to find Annie beside herself with anger over a situation in which her ex had caused great pain to her daughter – twelve years previously. Annie's friend stayed with her for two hours, listening to her and holding her while she wept. Eventually she managed to convince Annie that it was neither good nor helpful to be so angry and hurt about something that happened so long ago, and that she should seek counselling.

Within two months, Annie was a changed woman. After a series of sessions with a trained Christian counsellor, she found she was able to deal with her anger. She realised that she was hurting herself by holding on to her anger, and she was hurting the children, too, because when her extreme anger boiled over she would take it out on them. Her children – the very people she was angry with her ex for hurting! She acknowledged that she had no right to forgive on her daughter's behalf – that would have to be her daughter's choice. But she did learn to change her thought patterns so that she no longer raged about things that happened in the past and over which she had no control. She learned how to come to terms with the situation. These things had happened and nothing could alter it. She learned acceptance.

Forgiveness is a goal to be aimed for. It's a process which has to have a starting point. The act of forgiveness is too huge a step for anyone to take in a single stride. It's a difficult and draining path which requires many steps, and often it seems as if each step forward is countered by two steps back. At those times it's worth taking a quick look back to be reassured how far you have travelled. But only a quick look – don't dwell on the past again, or your steps back may start to mount up.

Being unwilling to forgive can only damage. Holding on to pain and resentment causes people to become bitter and self-centred. Being full of negative emotions is like a jug full of stale water; it has to be emptied out before fresh, clean water can fill it.

David's story

After at least six years of affairs with two other men, David's wife left him to cope alone with four children aged nine to fourteen.

He felt overawed by the prospect of having responsibility for all the cooking, cleaning, ironing and shopping, while holding down a job and dealing with the emotional needs of four children. He says he felt bewildered, angry and resentful. But his fear that he would not be able to survive and cope was matched with determination.

'I've kicked the cat a couple of times,' he admits. 'But only gently! My main concern was for the well-being of the children. Saying goodnight to my nine year old was a lengthy occasion full of questions and shared tears. I read a couple of books about children and divorce, and worried that the other three didn't seem to show any of the behaviours mentioned. Would they be harmed by keeping it all inside?'

He was particularly concerned for the children when they visited their mother. They would be upset when she had what he calls 'freak outs', and on some occasions they would run out and walk home. He tried to spend as much time as he could with them, often neglecting work and housework as a result. He tried to reassure them that it was all right to say, 'I love Mum but I don't like her.' He continued to take them for their weekly visit on Sundays, but although they were free to arrange to meet her at other times, they never seemed to want to.

'Each incident with their mother set us back a few paces in our efforts to lead as normal a life as possible,' he says. 'Sometimes I secretly wished she had died. At least there may have been some happy memories, and not this lingering anguish and pain.'

He kept much to himself, both practically and emotionally. He struggled with practical matters, but found it was easier to cope alone than to allow the help of 'some ladies' who offered to help and then tried to take over. He became weary of such help, as he did of those who suggested a broken marriage was 'six of one and half a dozen of the other'.

'I know no one is perfect,' says David, 'but I know in my heart I did everything to keep us together. Jane had no excuse for doing what she did. I honestly don't know what I could have done differently.'

As time went on, David learnt more and more practical skills. He found out how to sew, and what time to go to the supermarket to get the reductions. He discovered how not to become a doormat. 'The children soon learned to do their own ironing!' he says.

The question of forgiveness kept on coming up. David knew that life was too important to fill it with destructive feelings. The only way to go on was to forgive his wife. He felt he had done this but then was overwhelmed again with anger and bitterness. 'Forgiveness, for me, was a repetitive process,' he says. 'I thought I'd forgiven – then a difficult time at work, four requests for help with homework as soon as I opened the front door, another glance at the pile of ironing that grew by the day, and a mind still wondering what to cook for tea – these were the catalysts for "I shouldn't have to cope with all this on my own!"' But after several years, when old thoughts still surface, he is finally able to say, 'These things are forgiven.' They no longer have the power to taint and spoil, he says.

Now that he has taken early retirement, and the children are independent, David says he would love to have 'someone special to belong to'. But he knows that if he meets someone, he will have to work hard at trusting again. However wonderful they seem, he says the fear will lurk that they may change and go back on their commitment.

5

Where do I go from here?

The early days of bereavement are over, you're dealing with your emotions, and you've taken the first steps on the path of forgiveness. Now what?

Accepting the reality of your situation is a huge leap forward. It means you take stock of where you are right now, and you can look to the future, whatever it might hold. It means you can look at who you are, and begin to rebuild your self-esteem. It means you can even look outwards to other people's needs.

But when you accept that reality, you see the possible years and years of single parenting stretching before you. You come face to face with the dark hole of loneliness. How do you cope with long-term single parenting?

Ongoing problems

We asked twenty-seven single parents, predominantly Christians, about the ongoing problems they faced.

The problem which was identified more than any other was money, or rather, the lack of it. Twelve single parents, almost half those questioned, specified their main problem as uncertain finances, money difficulties or limited income.

Nine single parents, a third of the group, described their main ongoing difficulty as loneliness, aloneness or being alone. Three of them went further, and said they had an increasing longing for someone special to spend their lives with, a yearning for a close friend or a need for a partner.

Having time for everything (coping alone, managing a large workload, juggling work with family responsibilities) was one of the ongoing problems for eight of the twenty-seven parents.

Six said they were worried about the children's future, their behaviour or coping with their teenage years. Four said that seeing their ex-wife or ex-husband was a big problem. In two cases this was because it stirred up their emotions or love towards them. One was finding great difficulty in adapting from 'single parent' to 'single person' as the children grew up and left home. Another was anxious about whether or not she had the right to form a new relationship.

We will look in more detail at the three main ongoing problems, money, loneliness and time, which have been specified by the single parents themselves. Loneliness will be further explored in this chapter, and the more practical details of money and time will be examined in later chapters.

Facing singleness
How should you be facing the fact that you're single? First of all, what is 'single'? Everyone enters the world single and leaves it single. Even those who share a part of their time on earth in a close husband and wife relationship are still 'single' inside their own thoughts, and in their relationships with other people. Being married could be described as simply sharing our singleness.

Deep down, many single parents would like to marry again. It's natural to desire that intimacy, and it's honest to face up to the yearning for another relationship. But marriage isn't the answer for all problems; it isn't going to make everything all right. People who marry again take themselves into the relationship. They can't leave their own problems, hang-ups, hurt or pain behind. Some things are just as difficult whether people are married or single. For people to survive as single parents (whether or not they may marry in the future) they actually have to learn to be single, now. They can't live a temporary existence, on hold until they find another partner.

There are many organisations encouraging people in their marriage, helping them to deal with conflict and improve their relationship. But not only do people have to work at being married, they also have to work at being single. When people don't work at their marriages, they get in a rut, or start having real problems. The same can happen with single people; if they don't work at being single, they can get stuck and have problems. It involves effort, time and self-discipline. This might sound too much like hard work, but it's worth it in the end.

There are many misconceptions about singleness. Most of us have picked up these wrong images without even realising it, and they're lurking around in our subconscious minds. For example, you are too self-centred for anyone to live with; you have failed because you haven't been able to hang on to your partner; your marriage must have broken up because you are a domineering woman, a weak man, an unstable person; you are unfulfilled and are just waiting for a partner to give you some purpose; you are afraid of commitment. To this short list, many more misconceptions can be added, which play havoc with the single parent's self-image. When you think like this, you are actually saying that your present status is your fault; you are to blame for being single; you are a second-class citizen.

How you live and how you see your future depends on how you view yourself. Clearing out the misconceptions and accepting yourself are both part of coming to terms with the fact that 'I'm single, and I'm all right.'

Loneliness

'You can't be lonely – you're surrounded by your children all day long.' 'If you've got God, you need never be lonely.'

Recognise these sentiments? In response to anyone who has said such things to you, you may well say, 'What do they know about it?' Only you know how much you still long for some caring, human, adult company.

Thirty-two single parents told us about their feelings of loneliness. We asked them to describe in what circumstances they felt most lonely, how they felt and what helped them to overcome loneliness.

There were a great variety of answers as to when loneliness was at its height – or rather, its depth. But most of the answers appeared to fall into two categories: being alone, and being (in the words of one father) 'with people but on my own'.

The situation of being with other people cannot be avoided unless the single parent chooses to become a recluse. 'When I'm with a lot of couples, there is no one to whom I am important and no one cares whether I'm happy or sad,' one mother told us. 'I try to avoid situations where I know I'd feel lonely, like "couple" events or wedding anniversaries.'

Many others agree. 'It's bad when I'm at a social gathering and nearly everyone else seems to be with a partner. I feel empty, and as if a part of me is missing.' 'I feel bad mostly when I'm in a crowd. I feel that I don't fit in, I'm not normal. I feel isolation, envy, self-hatred and guilt.' 'When I go into church and I don't know where to sit, and at any big gathering where I see lots of couples, I feel as though I want to run home to a safe place.'

That feeling that home is safe is very common. Wanting to run away from crowds of other people, particularly couples, all of whom are perceived as being happy, is a natural reaction. We want to protect ourselves. They all have something that we haven't and it isn't fair, we tell ourselves. Perhaps they are worthy of it and we're not? We can even perceive them as all being better looking, much more fun and hugely more popular than we can ever be. Rushing home to our safe nests, we begin to feed on those thoughts.

Being alone is just as painful. 'It's worse in the evenings – I can't get out,' said one. And another, 'I'm lonely when I see an advert for a social event and know I can't go because there's no babysitter, no one to go with, no money and no transport.'

Several single parents found this aloneness particularly painful when their children were with the absent parent. One parent said, 'It's bad when I'm by myself for a weekend,' while another went further, 'I feel lonely when it's coming up to Bank Holidays – when my son sleeps at his dad's house and my daughter goes away for weekends – knowing I will be on my own. I feel no one wants me and I've nowhere to go.'

Mandy finds that neither of those situations worries her greatly, but there are two very specific times that she feels alone. One is when she wants to go on holiday and there is no one to go with. She has a close friend, Shelley, who would go with her, but Shelley's first priority is obviously to her own husband and children, and she can't manage two holidays. For Mandy to go alone with her son would be too lonely, she feels, so she prefers to stay at home.

The other situation that bothers Mandy is when she has practical problems in the house and doesn't have the skills to deal with them. Her ex was a DIY enthusiast, and could fix most things. Now she needs to phone a plumber, an electrician or a roofer – and not only do they cost money, she doesn't know which are trustworthy. Unless the problem is an emergency, she tends to put up with it. And get depressed.

Two of the parents we spoke with told us that the loneliness was particularly intense when they were ill, especially because they didn't know how the children would manage. But Annie put a different perspective on this. She pointed out that being ill as a single parent was better than being ill as an unhappily married woman. When she was married, people assumed that her husband would look after her, so didn't visit or inquire whether they could help. Her husband didn't care for her at all, and her loneliness then was intense. She remembers the slam of the front door as her husband left for work without saying goodbye, when she had flu and was lying in bed with a crying baby next to her and a child to take to school. But now she is a single parent, her friends know she will need help when she is ill, and she says she is much more supported than she ever was when she was married.

Annie is fortunate in having friends from her church who keep an eye on her. Other churches are not so sympathetic, or perhaps they just don't see what is in front of them. Joanna, for example, is very lonely and would love to go on a single parent holiday with her son, but cannot afford it. Her church has refused to help, because they need all their money for the roof and organ fund.

Katherine is disabled and has two children with special needs. When she went into hospital for cancer treatment, one family agreed to take her daughter for a week, but her other child went into care. A church member dared to say to her, 'When are you going to stop having problems?'

So what do our group of parents do about their loneliness? A majority said they were helped by a close relationship with God, through prayer and Bible reading. Sadly, a few had been hurt by the church and by the attitude of some other Christians. Although this had made them disillusioned with the church, it had strengthened their relationship with God. 'Reading my Bible helps, and having God's assurance of his great love for me,' said one. Another said, 'The knowledge that Christ knows what I feel and he understands really helps me. His grace is sufficient for me and he is with me always.'

The majority stress the importance of friends, with almost half saying they were helped by invitations, visits and going out. To have a close friend, or a group of friends, is a lifeline for those who parent alone. Many are helped by joining a group of single parents and being able to talk openly about issues with which others can identify.

The feeling that 'no one wants me', was often more of a state of self-pity than a reality, some admitted. One mother said that she knew there were plenty of friends out there who she could call on, but very often when she sat at home in a lonely heap, she just didn't want to pick up the phone. 'Later, when I admit to friends that I was feeling really low, they'll say "Why didn't you phone?" It's because I don't want to bother them, or perhaps I subconsciously want to be alone.'

There is a difference between being lonely and being alone. Many people like their own company, valuing the freedom of the time they spend alone. Annie says she turns down invitations for lunch on the Sundays her son is with his father, because she values the free time. Sometimes she decorates the house, at other times she does nothing very much. But she likes her own space.

Other people are made differently, and would grab an invitation to lunch with both hands. They hate being alone, and when their children are with their ex, they have to be in company. If you react like this, then on the days you cannot find the company, try to find a way of using your time positively. One single mother told us that when she found there was too much daytime without close companionship, she tried to set herself a task in the garden or house and aimed to accomplish it. Others said they developed hobbies or went for long walks, and one helped old ladies with their gardens and listened to them over a cup of tea.

As many parents explained, even after doing practical things and meeting other people, the inner loneliness persists. Being awake at two in the morning can be the loneliest time, and sleeping alone in the house can bring bad feelings. Knowing you're not totally alone helps, so meeting with other single parents, hearing their problems and sharing yours, can help. At least you know there are other people in the same boat.

Living a fulfilled life
How do you live a fulfilled life as a single parent? The key word here is relationships, as seen in some of the answers given above. People who live the most fulfilled lives as single parents have close relationships with others.

Relationships can be difficult for everyone. Human beings are self-centred, and relationships cause clashes. And for many single parents, it's particularly hard to become close to someone else because of the fear of rejection. It's easier to keep people at a distance; that way you don't get hurt. It's safer to keep a gap between you and everyone else. So you establish yourself as an island and surround yourself by sea, and you're too far away from the mainland for anyone to build a bridge over to reach you.

But as the poet John Donne said, 'No man is an island.' There may be strong support waiting for you out there, but you're not able to recognise it because you daren't risk getting too close, or to accept it because you're too frightened.

For those who have learnt to be islands on their own, ask yourself, 'Am I prepared to become vulnerable and to risk walking close to someone?' You need to be willing to learn to make better relationships with others, even though it means risk and cost, in order to be fulfilled and to move forward.

And remember, a relationship is a two-way activity. When you accept love and care from someone else, don't lose sight of the fact that there are others out there who could do with some love and care from you. It's not only single parents who lead vulnerable and stressful lives; everyone has their own pressures and difficulties. It may sound unfair to suggest that you care for other people when you're in need, or that you do something about your loneliness yourself, when you have so many things to do. But in reality that's how it works. As you reach out to others to meet their needs, you will find some of your needs being met too.

Carol's story

Fifteen years ago, Carol's husband went to live with another woman. He left her with two children, then aged nine and thirteen.

'I couldn't believe it, even though I knew the marriage wasn't good,' says Carol. 'I loved my husband so much, and couldn't understand why he left – although with hindsight I realise there were many contributing factors. I was totally devastated. I felt so hurt and rejected, and couldn't stop crying. Even now, fifteen years later, I'm still dealing with the pain. I'm still extra sensitive to rejection, no matter how remote, and personal relationships are still difficult. I find it hard to trust men or to become close to them.'

Because Carol had just taken up a new career, she was able to buy out her husband's share in the marital home. This made the budget tight, but she thinks it was worth it.

She found attitudes to divorcees unhelpful. 'Women view you as a threat,' she says. 'Then at the same time as I divorced, my sister-in-law became a widow, and my family were much more sympathetic to her than they were to me.'

She felt guilty because she had divorced her husband. 'I had vowed before God to love my husband. I divorced him. Therefore I felt I'd let God down. I felt totally alienated from God and the church. I couldn't pray, and I lost my faith. I felt I'd prayed for years for God to bless my marriage, and he hadn't (so I thought then); therefore if he didn't answer there was no God. I felt totally lost, and there was nothing worth living for. I kept going to church, but only for the children's sake.

'It took a long time to regain my faith, but when I did, it came back very personally. I had a lot of support from my home group, in particular one very close friend. Another couple, Brian and Helen, were very good to me and the children. Support still comes from the church.'

David, Carol's son, saw his father regularly, but her daughter Jenny chose not to. Jenny hated her dad, but this *wasn't just because he left, says Carol. 'The relationship had been poor before. She took her feelings out on her brother, but she was helped by Brian and Helen.*

'*My ex-husband's new partner didn't speak to David when he visited his dad. Initially, his dad didn't pay him much attention either, but left him to play with the two children he now lived with. Then when David realised that his dad was unhappy with his new partner, he found it difficult to reconcile the fact that the dad who he loved had made a mistake. He had to love him warts and all.*

'*I've loved the children and talked to them, but I've had many discipline problems over the years. They're both very independent, and both work out their own problems, often without talking to me about them. Jenny now lives with her boyfriend, and is sure she won't marry. David has had girlfriends, but he doesn't seem really interested.*'

Carol still deals with loneliness and not having someone close to share with. She has felt frustrated when she can't discuss family problems with someone who has deep knowledge of the circumstances. Going to help someone else is her way of coping with the loneliness. She says she has great understanding of people in her position, and is able to help both parents and children whose families have split up.

6

Managing your money

'Three out of five lone parents receive Income Support...One parent families are the fastest growing group living in poverty in Britain today.' (*National Council for One Parent Families*, 2001).

Not all single parents are struggling with money, but as we saw in the previous chapter, twelve of our group of twenty-seven lone parents cited money as their main ongoing problem. So how were these parents facing or solving the problem? Seven simply answered: prayer. The other five said they were working harder and being more economical; budgeting better; not dwelling on it, learning to accept the situation, and learning, with difficulty, to ask when there was a need.

Single parents learning to manage their money often have some amazing experiences. There are some who say they have experienced miracles – receiving a bill in the post that just cannot be paid, and finding in the second post an anonymous gift of exactly that amount. Miracles happen in other ways too. Denise used to receive her state benefit on Mondays, and always found it difficult to make it stretch for a whole week. One particular Saturday she had absolutely no money left, and no food for the following day. That afternoon, her dog escaped through the front door, and as she chased it down the road, she caught a £5 note which appeared to be fluttering towards her from the sky. 'That £5 was our Sunday lunch,' she says.

Those kinds of experiences are special. But no less important are the experiences of finding a need is immediately met once you make it known. Many parents have had the experience of, for example, discovering their washing machine is irreparable and mentioning it to a friend, who happens to know that another friend has just bought a new washer drier and is looking for a home for her old machine, which is not absolutely perfect but still in good working order.

Then there are those experiences of money stretching. On paper, you can't possibly get through to the end of the week, never mind the end of the month. And yet you do, but when you look back, you don't know how you did it.

Despite all these experiences, there's still a practical problem. Miracles don't happen every day of the week, and sometimes you're hard pressed to find the money you need. Your child's feet seem to grow more quickly than other children's do, you're sure the electricity bill appears more than once a quarter, and you can't put any more on the credit card because you know it won't be any easier to pay it off the next month. What practical things can you do?

Budget
Have you learned to budget well? You may have a vague idea that you've cut down all you can, but take a careful look. Learning to budget differently may mean changing spending priorities in order to pay crucial household expenses first. There may be something that

has become a habit (such as having a daily paper delivered) which is an extravagance at the moment. Reassess what you buy in the supermarket – and don't buy food on credit if you can possibly help it. There are several budgeting facilities available to help you spread the cost of paying bills, including stamps, key/card recharging, tokens and payment cards. Paying fuel bills each month through your bank account may mean you qualify for a discount.

It's particularly hard to adapt if, in your marriage, you've been quite well off. If you used to buy yourself and the children good clothes from high street shops, it will probably seem depressing to start looking in charity shops. But it can become exciting. In her well off days, Theresa used to buy her twins matching clothes from catalogues and baby clothes stores. As a single mother, she started visiting car boot sales (where she'd sell as well as buy!) and second-hand shops, and found it became a hobby. It gave her a boost to choose her garments, wash and iron them, see the twins dressed in them, and to know she'd got a bargain. She even found that doing her rounds of the charity shops threatened to become addictive, and she had to keep away unless there was something she really needed!

You may feel you don't have the skills needed to budget, or you may already be in the frightening situation of having debts mounting up. Contact your local Citizens Advice Bureau, or Credit Action (see address list). They will not only be able to help you sort out your budgeting, but will also be able to give guidance if you are in debt.

Ask

Is there any person or group you can ask when you're really in need? One of the twelve single parents who cited money as their main ongoing problem said her solution was learning, with difficulty, to ask for help.

It may be that someone – your mother, uncle, sister or a close friend – has made it clear that they don't want to offend you by giving you hand-outs but that if you really need help, the offer is there. Don't be too proud to take it.

There may not be anyone close to you who has offered help. If you're part of a church, club or group, try sharing your need with a leader or fellow member. Don't ask them to meet the need themselves; that could be embarrassing for you and for them, and if it's denied you'll feel rejected. Simply explain your financial difficulty and ask if they know of any way you can be helped over this temporary problem. It could be that they are able to approach the whole group with your need, perhaps keeping you anonymous, to find some support for you.

It's a very difficult thing to do. No doubt words spring to your mind, such as 'begging' or 'charity'. But if the roles were reversed, wouldn't you be willing to give to someone else in need? Asking for help doesn't mean you're weak, or that you're going to become dependent on other people for everything. It simply means that at this particular moment you have a need, and that life is going to be better for you and your children if that need is met.

Don't get used to this way of life, though. Once the specific need has been met, and you've bought the new shoes for your children or paid the electricity bill, don't ask for more help unless there comes another time when you really need it. If you go back for more when it's not strictly necessary, or waste what you're given, then not only will your supporter feel angry but you won't feel too good about yourself either. Keep your self-respect.

If you find a way you can give something back, too, you might feel better about receiving. You won't be able to do it in direct proportion, but if you've received a gift from someone, how about showing your appreciation by making them a cake on their birthday, or taking them a bunch of daffodils on a cold February day? And always remember to send a note to thank the person who has helped you, if you know who it is.

Share

Is there anyone with whom you can share costs? Single parent groups, or even a friendship between two single parents, can be good co-operatives. For example, you may be based at home with your children, and your car is unreliable. Another single parent you know goes out to work three afternoons a week, pays for after-school child care, and is good at car maintenance. What could be simpler than for you to collect her children from school on the three days she works, and in return she regularly services your car? Not only have you both saved money, but she knows her children are in good hands and you know your car is too.

Claim

Are you aware of all the benefits you could receive? Some people may be eligible to claim Working Families Tax Credit, for example, but simply don't know about it. There is a new benefit scheme for widows and widowers – the relevant booklet, NP45, comes with a claim pack. Your child may be able to have free school dinners, and help with the cost of school uniform and trips. Go to the Citizens Advice Bureau or DWP office and find out all you can.

Earn

Is there any way you could earn a little extra money? It's true that if you're already receiving benefits, you can only earn a small amount extra per week, and if you're already working, you may feel you have no time to do anything else. But there could be something you enjoy doing and find relaxing which would bring in a little more money. For instance, if you like sewing, you could make curtains for a friend. You may say you'd rather not accept money from a friend but if she bought you a couple of bags of groceries as a thank you present, would that be more acceptable?

To work or not to work?
This subject really needs a chapter in itself, if not a book! There are so many theories and strong beliefs on the subject. One single mother told us, 'I will support my family myself – the children will respect me for working to meet all our needs.' But another said, 'My children have already lost one parent – if I go out to work it will mean they lose both parents. They need me at home.'

There's a lot of guilt tied up in this debate, and too much judgment and condemnation. People on each side think they are right, and say so volubly. But single parents have enough to cope with, and they can do without the added guilt. There are two sides to every debate, and what is right for one won't be right for another.

An added complication to the debate is a gender issue. It is so often assumed that a single mother should stay at home and receive benefits, while a single father ought to go out to work and pay a childminder to look after the children. There are different expectations of men and women: a man's responsibility is to earn money, while a woman's place is with the children. There are some views that are so ingrained in our thinking that many people can't accept things any other way.

Of course, all these arguments also apply to two parent families. There's just as big a debate about working mothers in two parent families as there is in single parent families. But when it comes to working single parents, there are complications which don't apply so much to two parent families. The guilt that all working mothers carry to some extent is usually worse for the single mother, who is concerned that the children have been harmed enough already and that if she works it may be even worse for them. Then there's all the child care and housework which can't be shared with a partner; it all has to be done by the same parent who is earning the money, so tiredness and lack of time make it more difficult to go out to work.

Where does all that leave you, as you question what is right for your family? Some people reading this already know the answer for their situation, and it suits them. Others may feel they have no choice in the matter, and their only option is to work. But there are others who are struggling, not knowing if what they are doing is the right thing, or who haven't decided whether it's best for them to work or not. How should they decide?

There are three main issues to consider: money, your children and you. Can you afford to work or not to work? What's best for your children? And what is best for you? What do you actually want to do? These issues are usually so tied up that it's difficult to distinguish them but it will help if you can make the attempt.

Money

If you claim Income Support, you will be facing life without money to spare. You will be allowed to earn only a tiny bit extra before your benefit is cut. Some people think they have no choice; Income Support is so little that they can't afford not to work. On the other hand, you may be worse off if you take a job, depending on your earning capacity. There again, the introduction of Working Families Tax Credit has made it easier for single parents to return to work, particularly as it includes help with child care. By now you may be going round in circles, totally unable to figure out which option is best for you. Help is available – you now have the opportunity to explore your options with a New Deal Lone Parent Advisor at the Job Centre. If you make an appointment, you may even be pleasantly surprised at the benefits of going back to work. And the decision is always yours to make.

In addition to the purely financial side of the question about whether to earn money or receive Income Support, there are the individual's principles. One single parent said she went out to work because she believed benefits were designed to tide people over and to support those who were *physically* unable to work. As she was healthy and able to work, and her children were above the age of five, she believed it her duty to go out to earn her money. She also said her children were proud of her for working to support them, and that it gave them self-respect. Of course, there are many other single parents who would disagree, again on a matter of principle, saying that their role is to stay at home with the children: see the next section for more discussion on this.

List your income and outgoings if you go out to work, and your income and outgoings if you stay at home and claim Income Support. Remember to take into account tax and National Insurance, childminding costs, travel and additional clothes (which you'll probably need when you're out at work, instead of the jeans and T-shirt you wear at home). Weigh up the financial fors and againsts of going out to work.

The children
If you claim Income Support, you can be at home for the children. In the early days of single parenthood they will

be insecure and often traumatised. And as the years go on, they will still be very dependent on you. If you work, you'll have to leave the children with a childminder or nursery all day, or have them collected after school and cared for in the holidays. It could be that you're one of those fortunate parents who can find a decent job within school hours, but these are few and far between unless you're a teacher. And even then, you have to take into account the fact that you'll be extra tired and you'll still have all the chores to do once you get home, as well as the children's needs to deal with, plus the preparation to do at home ready for the next day at work.

On the other hand, you could be one of those people who thrive on a busy life, love your job and would be so bored at home that you're more likely to snap at the children if you're at home all day. Or you could feel that staying at home all the time might make you dwell on your situation and become increasingly depressed. Or you could believe, like the parent in the previous Money section, that your children would respect you and themselves more if you did work to support them. If any of these is the case, it could be better for the children if you go out to work.

Make another list of fors and againsts. Are your children so traumatised that they need you to be at home at the moment? Or are they adapting well to their changed circumstances, happy at school and secure in friendships outside the home? Do you have close friends or relatives nearby who can support them if you're not around?

You

Consideration of your own wishes and needs is usually the last priority on the list for the single parent. You're so busy thinking about what's best for the children that you don't stop to examine your own needs. But it shouldn't be like that. After all, if you don't look after yourself, your children will suffer anyway. So ask yourself: do I want to go out to work? Do I need to go out to work?

If you have a job you love or a career you feel is worthwhile and you want to be out there working, then that is as much a consideration as the needs of the children or the financial situation. Working may mean a boost to your self-esteem or a lift to your spirits. If working means you're also better off financially, that will also lift you. If it helps you to go out to work, then it could be the right thing for you. If it drags you down to go out to work, then you may be better staying at home.

Make your third list of fors and againsts, taking into account your own needs, desires and hopes for the future. You're quite likely to feel guilty and selfish when you do this but try to keep all other considerations out of the way, and concentrate on yourself.

Once you've compiled your three lists, take a good look at them. It could be that your Money and You lists tell you to go out to work, while your Children list tells you to stay at home, and you feel you're no nearer to making a decision than you were when you started. You may even find that there are equal numbers of fors and againsts, and you'll feel guilty if you stay at home and guilty if you go out to work.

No one else can tell you what to do: you'll probably receive conflicting advice anyway, which will confuse you even more. Talk it over with a close friend. It could be that as you speak out the possibilities to someone else, the answer becomes clear. You might find your answer in a great sense of peace about one of the options. And once you're as sure as you can be about what's right for you stick with it. Don't waste energy in constant worrying about whether you've made the right choice.

One final thought before we leave the subject of money. If you're short of it, you're probably going to do without things yourself. Once you've paid the bills, you make sure the children always come first. That's good. But do grant yourself the occasional treat. If you're given a gift of money, before you put it all into the general housekeeping fund, think about spending some of it on yourself. You are important, and it will help if you occasionally do or buy something just for you.

Liz's story

Liz knew something was very wrong with her husband, but didn't know what it was. She feared mental illness. When she actually heard the truth, that her husband had been having an affair, her initial feeling was relief.

But as the full implications of what was happening hit home, Liz says she began to wake up each morning with a sense of horror. Her husband left her to set up home with the 'other woman', who was Liz's friend and the mother of her elder son's best friend. Liz began to panic, cried through the night and was unable to concentrate.

She was jealous when her elder son, then eleven years old, visited his father. She feared losing his affection, and looking back she realises she tried too hard to please him. 'He's sometimes very demanding now,' she says. 'He got used to having his own way.'

She found it easier to accept contact visits once she tried to understand her children's feelings and to put them before her own. Talking to friends, in particular one couple who were very helpful in the early days, helped her to overcome the initial panic of becoming a single parent.

Liz contacted the children's schools, and they were treated sympathetically. They missed their father terribly, and Liz feels her ex could have made more effort with their eight year old son. 'He didn't fit in to the new family because he was younger,' she says, 'and he wasn't included in their family holiday. He didn't feel welcome at their house and he stopped going. Things are better now, although he still has less contact than my elder son. There's an open invitation to them to visit whenever they want to, and occasional more definite invitations on special occasions. They both seem to have accepted things now; either that, or they're reluctant to talk about it. I've tried not to criticise their father, or what he has done. Recently I've been able to talk more deeply about relationships, and I've explained that I was too dependent in my marriage.'

Money was tight in the early days, but soon Liz found a job, and with a loan from her father she bought a car. She learnt to be more confident about driving and finding her way around, to manage her finances and to do minor repairs and decorating. She discovered she could be capable and independent when she had to be, and says it felt good to be in control of her life. At the same time, she found there were limits to what she could do well, and began to accept herself when she failed.

She says she also had to face up to and accept forgiveness for some of her earlier mistakes. This has made her less judgmental towards her ex-husband, and has made it easier to forgive him.

'But I'm still sometimes afraid that if people get to know the real "me" too well, they will turn away,' she says. 'That's what has seemed to happen several times in my life.'

7

Organising your time

You're managing the home, children, finances – and holding down a job. You're learning new juggling skills as you keep work and family responsibilities in the air at the same time. Where do you find the time for everything? When you can't do everything at once, what do you do first? What do you let go, when you can't cope with all you have to do? And where do you find time for yourself?

There's another side to the time problem. There are single parents who don't go out to work, and find they have too much time on their hands. They're at home all day with the children, or while the children are at school they wake each morning and see another length of hours stretching ahead, with nothing to fill them but memories, doubts, boredom, depression. What do they do with their time?

Look at the daily diaries of two lone mothers.

Suzanne's day
7.00 Alarm goes off. Go downstairs and make a cup of tea. Feed the cat. Make the children's lunchboxes. Take a shower. Have breakfast with Joe and Alice. Put a load of washing into the machine.

8.20 Leave the house. Drop the children at school. Drive on to work.

9.00 Arrive at work. Long day typing, organising, taking minutes, answering phones, with hardly any break. I have an arrangement with my employer that if I only take a half-hour lunch break instead of an hour, I can leave half an hour earlier, so I arrive home just after the children.

4.30 Leave work. Arrive home and spend time with Joe and Alice, catching up on their day at school and preparing a quick meal together.

5.15 Eat tea, then drop the children off at their friend's house and drive on to the supermarket where I work three evenings a week to supplement my income.

8.30 Finish work, fill a basket of shopping (mustn't forget loo rolls tonight – we're using a box of tissues at the moment because I forgot last night), pay for it at discount rate – a great bonus for us.

9.00 Collect Joe and Alice, drive home and send them off to get ready for bed. Alice says she forgot to take her schoolbag to their friend's house, so she still hasn't done her homework for tomorrow. I tell her she'll have to get it done in bed. Empty the washing machine, take dry clothes off the clothes horse, hang up the wet ones, go up to say goodnight to the children, iron the dry clothes.

10.00 Put away last night's washing up, which has spent twenty-four hours on the draining board, wash up today's things and leave them to dry. Joe appears downstairs to say he forgot to tell me his teacher says I must send £5.00 for the school trip no later than tomorrow. Get annoyed with Joe, raid my purse, find £3.72, decide to leave earlier tomorrow to drive round by the hole in the wall. Comfort Joe who says it's not his fault.

10.25 Switch on TV for the end of *News at Ten*, but don't really listen to it because at last I've got time to open the post that arrived this morning. A final demand for the phone bill, and a reminder that the TV licence needs renewing at the end of the month. Consider whether to give up the TV – we hardly ever have time to watch it. A lovely letter from a friend, saying she hopes I'm all right, as I haven't replied to her last two letters. Cheers me up, but also makes me feel horribly guilty.

10.45 Decide to write a letter straight back, but notice the dust everywhere, and remember we have visitors at the weekend. Hover between writing-pad and duster, decide I'm too tired to do either, and go to bed.

Sheila's day

8.15 Sam wakes me up, and I find we've got to leave for nursery in twenty minutes. Tell Sam to get himself dressed while I make his toast. Decide my coffee can wait until I get back. Get myself dressed and walk him to nursery.

9.00 Buy a paper, get home, make coffee, read the paper.

10.00 Make another coffee, eat three biscuits, watch a chat show on TV.

11.00 Decide I must get moving. Put some washing in the machine, think about making a shopping list, but I lack enthusiasm for this as we always get the same things anyway.

11.30 Phone a friend. She's out. Phone another. She's in, and I ask her round for lunch. That gives me incentive to go shopping on the way back from collecting Sam. Treat myself to some French bread and cheese for our lunch, as well as the usual things.

1.00 Friend arrives, and we spend a couple of hours putting the world to rights. Sam plays around us, asking us things now and again.

3.20 She leaves to collect her children from school. I watch all the children's programmes with Sam, then he watches *Neighbours* with me.

6.00 Make beans on toast for tea.

6.30 Play two games of Ludo with Sam.

7.15 Bath Sam and put him to bed. Put on his nappy because he still wets the bed even though he's four and at the nursery of his big school. I'm told it's nothing to worry about until he's seven. Read him a bed-time story.

8.00 Come downstairs. There's nothing good on TV tonight, but I watch it anyway.

10.00 Really tired, although I don't know why. Remember I put some washing in the machine this morning, but decide to let it stay there until tomorrow. Go to bed.

Two mothers with very different problems. Suzanne hates having to rush around so much, with the double pressures of having to earn enough money to support her family and not having enough time with the children. She never seems to have time for herself, either. She's unhappy with her situation, but can see no alternative.

Sheila appreciates the fact that she's at home for Sam, but she has too much time on her hands, and is unable to find the motivation to use it well. She feels guilty that she sits around, watching TV, chatting to friends, getting bored. She knows the time she spends with Sam is hardly ever the quality time the magazines talk about. She's unhappy with her situation, but doesn't know how to change it.

Too much time on your hands
Maybe you've decided that going out to work isn't financially viable, or perhaps you believe you should be

at home for the children. Do you find, like Sheila, that you haven't enough things to do? You may feel depressed and lack motivation even to clean the house or go shopping. Or, you may have a spotless and well-organised house, do your shopping, mending and ironing daily but find that when you've done all those things you still have too much time to fill.

Stop and think what you would like to spend your time doing, given your circumstances. If the children are at school, you have no term-time childminding problems. Consider attending classes to learn new skills, to gain a qualification, or just to study for its own sake. Some adult colleges allow students to go in and use the computers on a teach yourself basis. It costs nothing. Others offer a whole term's classes for the unemployed at a greatly reduced rate. Find out what your local college offers.

Or you might like to do some voluntary work, for example at an Oxfam shop or a local church café. Think about people you could visit, not only your friends, but the housebound or disabled who would appreciate some company. You wouldn't just be passing the time through doing these things, you'd be helping yourself, helping others, finding new interests and making new relationships.

If your children are pre-school age, find out about local drop-ins, toddler groups, under-fives clubs or branches of organisations like Gingerbread or Care for the Family's single parent support. To find out what's available, look in the local free newspaper or ask your health visitor or clinic. Plan your day, trying to include at least one outside activity, whether it's a trip to the park, shops or a club or just a walk to the post office in the rain. You may think home activities with pre-schoolers are tedious, or feel you're no good at the practical, messy games that children love but if you could manage to plan a half-hour painting session or a dressing-up game, you would all benefit from it. However, don't only find things to do with your children, look for something you can do for yourself. Spending even one morning a week at the local adult education college can make a huge difference to you. Even if there's no one you feel you can leave the children with for a morning, the college will probably run a crèche where your children can stay while you attend a class.

Starting something new takes motivation and energy which you may feel you lack. It also takes confidence, something many single parents don't have. But getting started will probably be the hardest part. To help you begin, try making a timetable for your week. It will aid motivation, lessen the guilt about what you're not doing, and give you a sense of achievement when you see what you have done. It also gives structure to the week, an important element which gives different patterns to different days and stops you from feeling you're drifting aimlessly.

Into the timetable you might put, for example, half an hour's housework each morning, or a room per day, followed by the reward of a cup of coffee. On Mondays you could do most of the week's washing, and catch up with letter-writing; Tuesday could be ironing in the morning and toddler group in the afternoon; Wednesday, shopping, library visit, then an evening class. It sounds a little like life in Grandma's day but it works.

If you can summon up the courage to begin, you will almost definitely find that motivation, energy and confidence will follow, growing stronger as you go on.

Not enough time
At the other end of the scale are single parents like Suzanne, who, far from not having enough things to fill

their time, have too little time to do everything that needs doing.

Eight of the group of twenty-seven parents (see Chapter 5) told us that finding time for everything, now they are on their own, is one of their main ongoing problems. None had found a solution. Only one mentioned something which helped practically: she said she had learnt how to say no to some things. But of course this didn't solve everything. So what are stressed, overworked lone parents to do?

First, face your situation. Recognise the signs of stress in yourself. Don't keep saying, 'I'm only busy and everything is perfectly all right; so long as I can just keep going, I'll be fine.' Admitting you're under stress doesn't mean you're a failure. Acknowledge that you're coping alone with all the practical things – going to work, caring for the children, cleaning, washing, ironing, shopping, cooking. Add to this the shock or grief you're still feeling because of the divorce or death of your partner, the pain you're feeling for your children, the loneliness you're coping with, as well as the money worries or lack of understanding you may be facing because you're a lone parent. You may wonder how you still keep going at all!

But once you've looked at your life, don't get into a state of self-pity. You may not be able to rid yourself of stress by giving up work or never doing the cleaning again, but you can learn to care for yourself within your circumstances. Assuming you can't change your working pattern (arranging more flexible hours, for example) and you can't afford a cleaner, what can you do to organise your time and make changes?

To start with, keep a diary of your free time. There are many hours in the day (usually during the week unless you're a shift-worker) which can't be changed. You're at work, then cooking the dinner, then putting the children to bed. Not much can be changed there. But there are other hours (for most people, evenings and weekends) in which you could make better use of your time and ease your stress.

Keep a diary of a typical week. Write down what you did with your evenings and weekend, and how long each thing took. Then analyse your findings. Did you spend so much of the weekend relaxing that you didn't achieve anything? On the other hand, did you rush round madly trying to fit in everything possible and please everybody, and have no time to relax? Either way, you had an unbalanced weekend. You could have found ways to plan your time so you could both relax and achieve something. How can you decide how to plan that time?

Be realistic. You have enough to cope with at the moment. If there's anything you're doing that isn't essential, and can be done by someone else, then offload it. Decide what is most important to you, and stick with that.

Start saying no. If someone asks you to help with the catering for a special community event on Saturday, for example, don't feel you really ought to say yes. If you're busy all week, and you think Saturday is a precious day to be with the children and to catch up on housework, then you must learn to say no.

Plan your time with the children. Asking 'How much time should I spend with the children?' is like asking 'How long is a piece of string?' Your children, of course, need you to be with them, and in one sense any time spent with the children is well spent. You are at least physically together. But if spending time with the children means you all sit around and hardly speak to each other, is that time well spent? Wouldn't it be better for you to plan to do certain activities together for some of the day or evening, which you could enjoy as a family, and then arrange some time for yourself?

Let the children help. Do you take on everything yourself, even though your children are old enough to help? If you think you're doing the children a service by doing everything for them, then think again. Allow your children to share household responsibilities with you. Don't tidy their bedrooms, make their beds and collect their washing for them, if they're capable of doing it themselves. If they're old enough to iron or to cook a meal, why not let them do it? They'll probably enjoy it, and it will take the pressure off you. If you work together, it also means you have more time with them. As single father Edward says, 'When a man is left with children to raise and a job to hold down, he's intensely tired. However, with teenagers there is often a sense of pulling together, and pride in tasks well done. Make a rota of tasks, and give rewards for exceptional help.'

Don't keep up appearances. Are you houseproud, and stressed because you haven't time to keep the house as spotless as you used to? Did you use to fill in every bit of paperwork immediately, pay the bills before the red one arrived and return phone calls within the hour, and now you're letting things slide because there's no time? Did you leave the house every morning in newly washed and ironed clothes, and now you feel ashamed because you often wear things you haven't had time to iron? Ask yourself, do any of these things really matter? Make allowances for yourself. If you're holding down a job and caring for the children, you can be proud of yourself. A few creases or a little dust are unimportant compared to the giant task you are undertaking. Don't add to your stress by worrying about unnecessary things.

Make lists. You may think you're not the list-making type, but try it anyway. If you get yourself organised, it's surprising how much more can be achieved in a little time. Write shopping lists and try to do as much shopping in one go as you can, rather than picking up a few things on the way home from work, finding you've forgotten something crucial and having to go back the next day. Make 'to do' lists for home, and for children's school and leisure activities (sew on Tim's name tapes, buy Alison new trainers, find out when the next second-hand uniform sale takes place, arrange someone to collect Tim from Scouts' bonfire on Thursday, fill in medical forms).

Get support. If you're struggling on your own, then get help. It may mean admitting you're in need, but don't be frightened of that. People can and do respond, and it's nothing to be ashamed of. You may need practical support in the home or with child care, or you may just need a shoulder to cry on. There will be one out there. Look for it.

If you're out at work, let your boss and colleagues know of the family situation. Most will be understanding. It's important, not only because the emotional upheaval is likely to affect performance, but also so that sympathetic colleagues will be able to give assistance on days which are particularly difficult.

Decide to go out at least one evening a week. Plan a regular meeting with a friend to have a treat. If you don't think you can afford to eat out, see a film or go to the gym, just go to their house, or get together with a larger group of friends. Determine to get a babysitter and have that time for yourself. Don't give in to exhaustion for that one evening. The ironing can wait until tomorrow, and you'll probably feel less exhausted because you made the effort.

Learn to relax. If you can't unwind at all, you're going to feel more stressed, ill and unable to sleep at night. And you need your sleep. If you don't know any relaxation skills, find out from your GP. Try to spend at least ten uninterrupted minutes every evening sitting alone, quietly, without the TV or the children. You may choose to spend that time thinking, praying or simply doing nothing at all. Or you may like to play some soothing music. Whatever you do, it's an opportunity to stop for a while.

Whatever your situation, whether it's too much or too little time on your hands, don't be afraid to make changes. The first change you make will be the most difficult. Try to think positive. If you can manage to lift yourself out of a bored rut, or learn to cope better with your overworked, stressed existence, then confidence and renewed energy will follow.

Hazel's story

When Hazel's parents divorced in the late 1960s, her mother became emotionally and physically unstable. This seriously affected her ability to care for her five children alone.

During her teenage years, Hazel felt isolated, lonely and angry. She sought solace and success through her music lessons at school, dreaming that she would make music her career. When her mum told her that she had to go out to work, she was horrified. She tried many ways to find the love she was desperate for, and at the age of nineteen she purposely became pregnant, believing that would finally fill the void. But parenting was not the answer, and she soon went back to her promiscuous lifestyle.

Hazel's daughter, Emma, spent much time with family and friends. She didn't know who her main carer was, and the bonding between mother and child did not take place. Hazel did not consider Emma's father to have any role in her life, and he returned to his own country when Emma was four months old.

When Hazel was twenty-three, a male friend who was unable to set up a business because of visa restrictions asked her to help. She agreed to allow all the business and financial responsibility to be put in her name. But she received nothing. In 1986 her DSS payments were stopped because she was classed as owning a business. She had no money for food or bills. The gas and electricity were cut off. Hazel sold her furniture and personal items to live.

Her family washed their hands of her, and no help was forthcoming from the Citizens Advice Bureau, a solicitor, the DSS, Social Services or the local newspaper. She remembers four year old Emma crying, 'Please Mummy, when are we going to get better?' Cold and hungry, they walked for four hours through the snow to reach a friend.

This friend introduced Hazel to the pastor of her church, who offered to come and listen to her. She was amazed that he returned one hour later to say that he had arranged a free meeting with a solicitor later that day. From then on she received practical support, and life changed for the better. Hazel asked the pastor why he was helping someone he did not know and who had no money. 'The pastor said God loved me,' says Hazel. 'Me, a liar and a cheat who had no regard for others. I believed him and then I believed God and gave my life to him.'

The past sixteen years have not been easy, but Hazel says she got through with the help of her church and Care for the Family, who accepted, guided and encouraged her. 'Without them I would not have built a loving, caring relationship with my daughter, who is now twenty and at college,' she says. 'Nor would I have studied for a diploma in child care and be working now with the Child and Family team of Social Services. God and others cared enough for me, despite the way I lived my life, not to leave me there.'

8

Sexuality, intimacy and remarriage

If you look at most films, commercials and magazines, you'd think the only way to exist was as one half of a couple. The media, reflecting society (or perhaps society reflecting the media?), says that to be alone is not normal. Living in a world with these values can be a problem to all single people. And for the single parent who has been used to being part of a couple, adapting to the world of singleness all over again is even more difficult.

Added to this is the deep need of every human being to be loved and accepted by a partner, to be intimate with one other person emotionally and sexually. Both outer pressures and inner needs cry out to the single parent – get yourself a partner!

But life isn't like that. New partners can't be found growing on trees, and even if they were, there's no guarantee that there's a Mr or Ms Perfect out there with whom you're going to live happily ever after. You may feel better about yourself with a partner by your side, you may think you'll feel whole again if you're half of a pair. But rushing into any relationship out of loneliness isn't an answer.

Facing the fact that you are single – and that it's possible you may remain so – was one of the issues explored in Chapter 5. Once you've accepted that fact you're over half way there. But you still have to live with the pressures of the world, your need for intimacy and the sexual desires which may all but eat you up at times.

Many newly-single parents rush into a sexual relationship with another partner. As one single father says, there's a danger of promiscuous behaviour as a reaction to grief, a desire for revenge on a partner or in an attempt to overcome intense loneliness. There's also the need for reassurance that they are still attractive to someone else. When people feel lonely and their self-image is poor, they think that having sex with someone will fulfil their needs and make them feel good. But sex is not an end in itself. It's more than likely they'll find any good feeling will be short-lived. If they felt used and rejected in their marriage, they'll feel even more used and rejected by having sex with a person who is not committed to them.

Christians believe that sex is intended to be part of a complete, giving, committed relationship; the ultimate expression of love within marriage. People who hold this view, and believe therefore that they should remain celibate until they marry again, also have to face the possibility that they may not marry again. If you are one of those people, struggling to hold on to spiritual and moral principles, can there be a fulfilling and satisfying future? Is there a substitute for sex?

It would be easy to churn out platitudes and clichés on the subject of sexuality. But ducking the issue isn't going to help anyone. As one single mother says, 'I miss the warmth of a close physical relationship but find that it's taboo in the church to even talk about having sexual feelings! I once attended a singles group where we were meant to be discussing our difficulties honestly, and I was struggling with this problem. The reaction was, "Oh, you need prayer. We don't have feelings like that." I never did find anybody to talk to about it. Nobody admits to the need.'

Carol had had a good sex life with her husband. In the years after he died, she told us she had 'an overwhelming desire to find release', and she often masturbated. Eventually she came to a point where she found this such an inward activity that she stopped. Many people feel guilty, dirty and often even more lonely after they've masturbated. But while it's self-centred, it isn't at all abnormal. The time to worry is when it becomes so compulsive that it overtakes everything else. For those who feed fantasy by buying pornographic magazines and choosing the company of those magazines night after night instead of any other activity, a fulfilled life really isn't possible. Seriously asking themselves what they're getting out of it and what they really want out of life might be the first move in stopping the addiction.

Much of the advice given on how to deal with sexual feelings can be suggestions to take a cold shower or push the feelings down. But this sort of counsel denies sexuality. The fact is that everyone is a sexual being; their sexuality didn't die when their marriage did. There has to be a more constructive way of dealing with it.

Some people use sublimation as a way of dealing with sexuality. To sublimate doesn't involve squashing down feelings. According to the dictionary, it means, 'Transmute into something nobler...direct energy of (primitive impulse) into activity socially more useful or regarded as higher in cultural or moral scale.'

Feelings can be channelled into creative tasks in the home, with the children, in work or leisure activities. Parents could look at ways of redecorating their home more creatively, getting ideas from design magazines. Or they could take up tennis or running, things they may not have done since pre-children days. Even something as simple as setting up a creative new filing system at work can seem exciting, if enough energy and imagination is put into it. The creative energy can flow, and they can find themselves happier, more fulfilled and more energetic than they have been for years.

Of course, the feelings will come and go. There will still be bad days, when the creativity of making a farm out of cardboard boxes with young children – or even planning to climb all the Scottish mountains or start flying lessons – will seem pointless and banal. On those days, the feeling of 'I just need a partner and nothing else will do' will be paramount. But those times should become less frequent than they once were. And keeping so busy during the day not only gives a great sense of achievement but also means people go to bed exhausted, which also means they may often appreciate the comfort of a single bed and the chance to sleep.

Kathryn knew that her attempt to use sublimation to build a new way of life would provoke cries of 'You must be joking!' But after years of experience, she says it is possible to live a fulfilled life without a sexual relationship. However, she says her fulfilment didn't only involve pouring her energy into new activities and hard work. It also meant keeping away from films, books or magazines which would stir up desires and make her dissatisfied with her present life. When you're on a diet, gazing longingly at a baker's window full of cream cakes isn't going to help. You may love cream cakes, but you're trying to do without them. Transformed alcoholics aren't going to be helped by keeping a whisky bottle on the table, and having a quick peek at it every time they walk past. They may long to have a drink but they know they can't have one so why provoke the desire? It may sound negative at first ('Don't think about it!') but in reality it's positive. If they threw away the whisky and found other things to take its place (started a self-help group or learnt a new skill at evening class) they'd be much happier.

Finding other creative and fulfilling activities doesn't mean people have to deny their sexuality, in fact it means quite the opposite. Some people try to hide from the opposite sex; women dress dowdily, never consider colouring or re-styling their hair; men just don't bother. But it's important not to lose one's femininity or masculinity. It's part of staying creative and being an individual, and is in itself an expression of sexuality. People's choice of clothes, hairstyle, colour, fashion – like their choice of decor, gifts, food, friends – is an expression of their personality and individuality. Just because they're not taking part in regular acts of sex, it doesn't mean they're sexless. They have a sexual identity, and it needs to be expressed.

For some single parents, having a very close friend is a great compensation for the lack of a sexual partner, and it can provide a warm, affectionate, non-sexual relationship.

Having friends with whom you drink coffee, share meals and see films is fine, but unfortunately, most friendships stop there. You may enjoy a chat, even exchange personal thoughts and feelings, but you wouldn't describe yourself as 'close'. The human need for affection and closeness can often be confused with the need for sex. Finding a close friend can fulfil this need. So how can a friendship be close, or intimate, without being sexual?

Elaine and Sarah had been friends long before they met their husbands. Although Sarah's marriage was happy, Elaine's wasn't, and she came to depend on Sarah as someone she could confide in and draw support from.

Elaine began to worry that her feelings for Sarah might be sexual. She didn't believe they were and yet she knew her feelings could only be described as love. It took a couple of years before she realised that Sarah was fulfilling a need that wasn't being met by her husband, but it wasn't a sexual need. With Sarah, she had a loving relationship, without sex; with her husband, she had a sexual relationship without love.

In her sorrow at the knowledge that her marriage was breaking up, Elaine was at a stage when it wasn't sex she needed, but support, security, respect, affection, warmth, trust – all things she was lacking in her relationship with her husband. She realised that there was an ideal, in a completely full, intimate, sexual relationship, but if she had to choose between an intimate and a sexual relationship, she knew she would choose intimacy.

Intimate friendship is what a marriage should provide, and does for some people but all too often doesn't for others. It's possible to have a close relationship without sex. The two shouldn't be confused, and if a person finds real closeness, they should keep hold of it, without thinking it means they're obliged to jump into bed.

There are dangers in becoming too close to a member of the opposite sex, of course. The story goes something like this: a single mother receives support from another couple, the husband helps her particularly with jobs around the house, she comes to depend on him, he's having problems in his own marriage, before long they have become an 'item'. It's for this reason that some married women are wary of their single friends, and dislike their husbands helping them. That in itself can be hurtful to the single mother, but it's understandable.

Single parents need to be aware of their vulnerability. They are in need of love and support, and it's easy to allow themselves to slip into a relationship that they didn't mean to start. Their vulnerability can also stem from the fact that after being hurt in their first marriage, they don't believe they're attractive any more so they don't even realise someone finds them so. Anna says, 'I didn't realise I was on shaky ground, I felt completely innocent, and simply glad I had a male friend who was willing to help me. I told myself there was no problem. But before long I started depending on him, longing for his visits. Then I realised he'd started to feel something for me too. I didn't go looking for it – it just "happened". I was in a terrible situation, hurting another family as well as my own, and having to get out of it was almost as painful as my marriage breaking up.'

Even if a single parent finds someone who is available (i.e. of the opposite sex and not married), they should still be aware of their vulnerability. Some lone parents have told us that even an innocent date unleashes a whole load of emotions. They found it was like being a teenager again, with all the mood swings, uncertainty, shyness and excitement. It's easy to believe 'this is it!' but it might not be anything more than a brief acquaintance or the start of a good friendship. Appreciate what is offered, don't anticipate immediate permanent commitment.

It's important not to rush into another relationship too quickly, before there has been a recovery from the first. The foundations for building a second marriage are much stronger for those who have come through the grieving experience, have learnt from their past rather than seeing it as something that is bound to be repeated, and have come to know and like themselves as 'complete' single people.

Some people view remarriage with hope and joy; others are full of fear. If they've been through one broken relationship, they're likely to fear trusting someone again, fear being hurt, fear that they'll fail. They go through the pendulum swing, from 'I can never trust anyone again' to 'I can't face the rest of my life on my own.' In remarrying, they're taking a risk, but every relationship is a risk. Talking to their new partner about their fears will probably result in discovering that they are feeling the same way. For those with really strong fears (associated with abuse or rape in their previous relationship, for example) it's important to seek professional help before they attempt to start all over again.

There are several considerations in a second marriage that weren't there first time round. Anyone seriously considering remarriage should ask themselves:

- Why do I want to remarry? Do I really love this person, yearn to be with them all the time, and want what is best for them? Or do just I want someone to love me, to take responsibility, to be a parent for my children, to keep me company?
- My past won't be wiped out by remarrying. Have I come to terms with it and learnt from it? Do I need help in understanding my own past before I marry again?
- Am I remarrying just to get back at my first partner?
- My new partner isn't my children's natural parent. Do I believe s/he will be a good parent to them, and is this remarriage the best thing for my children? My new partner has children too. Do I really want to take them on as well? Can I learn to love them?

There are potential negatives to remarrying. But for many people there are huge positives. After a disastrous first marriage, Ted found that Liz became a supportive and loving second wife who was much more of a mother to his children than their real mother had been. Liz came from an abusive first marriage, and it took some time for her to accept that Ted really was going to treat her differently. There were many difficulties in the early years, particularly arguments over the children from both marriages (when 'his' sons and 'her' son hadn't yet become 'our' sons), problems over contact arrangements with their first partners and financial worries. But twenty years on, and now both in their late fifties, they are happy and secure, and Ted is clearly as much in love with Liz as he was when he first met her. The past is not bound to be repeated.

Sheila's story

*Sheila's husband had his first heart attack when their son
Charles was two years old. A year later, he asked to take early
retirement due to continuing ill health, and Sheila returned to
work. She says she quickly 'got into career mode'. By the time
Charles was seven, his father had had his third heart attack. It
is unusual to survive the third, and doctors told him that his
heart was like a pump that would gradually wear out.*

*'For a year, we watched him fade away,' says Sheila. When
he died, Charles was eight years old, and Sheila was also left
with a step-daughter of nineteen and a twenty-one year old
step-son. One year before, they had been a family of five; suddenly there were only two of them living at home. Clare was
at university, and Sheila and her husband had encouraged
John to leave home as they didn't want him to feel responsible
for the family after his father died.*

*After the long illness, Sheila was relieved that her husband
had died; she says it was what he wanted. But she felt numb,
and only coped in the early days by following instructions
from friends and family. She began to feel guilty that she had
failed as a wife, and felt she should have had more sympathy
with her husband. She tried to continue to do things in the
way he wanted – he had left full instructions regarding money
affairs. It was four years before she recognised his house as her
own.*

*Her children lost 'the parent who sat and listened,' says
Sheila. 'I did nothing to help them – I was too wrapped up in
my own feelings at the time.'*

*She feels she made matters worse for her children by getting
seriously involved with another man fifteen months after her
husband's death. 'It was too soon,' she admits. 'I was trying to
replace my husband.'*

*She became engaged, and the date was set for the wedding.
Then her fiancé broke off the engagement and quickly became
engaged to someone else. 'It was like a divorce,' says Sheila.*

'The pain of rejection was much worse than the grief of death. The loss also affected Charles deeply – my fiancé had become his father-figure, and is still his memory of a father.

'We discuss all these things now, and there is evidence that healing is taking place. We try to be open about our lives and feelings, but this is more difficult with the boys. My step-daughter helps conversation along.'

When Charles started secondary school, he was seen as a child with problems, due to coming from a single parent family. 'Actually, his problems were very similar to his brother's, but the difference was that then I had a husband to visit the school with me,' says Sheila.

Clare suffered with terrible depression four years after her father's death. 'It was discovered she was grieving for her mother, who had died when she was fourteen months old,' says Sheila. 'She didn't know who she was. She had been brought up with my standards and ideals, and when she saw her maternal family, they were quite different. She almost felt guilty that she had turned out "better" than them, and that her grandmother was so proud of her. We are very close, even though she now lives miles away. Her brother, John, is more like their mother and he fits in with both families, although he is so quiet I find it hard to communicate with him.'

Over the first few years after she became a widow, Sheila says it was only her church connections that held her together. One friend in particular was like a mother, and was always there for her. Then another single parent joined the church, and for a few years they went on holiday together. The downside of church life was that several people now saw her as a free agent, and gave her jobs to do – but no babysitter.

Gradually, she learnt to cope alone, to take responsibility for the practicalities of life, and is particularly proud of being able to manage the house inside and outside. She continued to miss someone to share the load in practical ways, and still finds that there is not enough time to do all that needs to be done. She *learnt to deal with loneliness, which hit her especially hard when her son became a teenager and began to rebel. 'Then, as my son reached his late teens, he became the man of the house and started to dominate me,' she says. 'Fortunately, as the youngest of three, he is pulled into line!'*

Is life any different for a lone parent who is single because she has been widowed? 'In my church widows are "respectable", and are not viewed in the same way as women with children on their own through divorce or being unmarried,' says Sheila. 'They don't usually have such a hard time financially, provided they are willing to subsidise their pension with earnings. I would think there are fewer widows with children in the poverty trap.

'Widows don't have the trauma of rejection. The child knows that his father did not choose to leave him – death is a natural process which comes to us all. On the other hand, my son was quite jealous of his friend whose parents were divorced, as his friend was able to see his father and talk to him on the phone.'

9

Helping children through their loss

All the time you are coping with your loss and grief, your children are going on their own journey of bereavement. It takes time for them to work through their loss too. At the very time you feel least able to deal with their pain, they need you. There will no doubt be many times when you feel you've let them down, not been there for them or been so full of your own pain that you didn't recognise theirs. But there will be other times when you can listen to them, help them and find the right, comforting words to say to them.

Melanie says she was a rational, loving, caring mother before her husband left. Once she was alone with the children, there were times when she didn't recognise herself. 'I would lash out and scream at the children even though they'd done nothing to deserve it,' she says. 'I would get carried away and become perfectly unreasonable. I could see myself behaving irrationally, as if I was watching myself on film, and yet I couldn't do anything to stop it. The children were being hurt, and I hated myself, but I was out of control.'

The things that sparked off Melanie's emotional outbursts were phone calls or visits from her ex-husband.

He might phone to arrange to collect the children at the weekend, and the call would deteriorate into a slanging match. Or he'd bring the children home after a weekend, and there'd be a hissed exchange of abuse in the hallway. When he'd gone, Melanie would let all her emotion out in front of the children.

But even though Melanie was feeling an emotional tidal wave of guilt, rejection, anger and hurt, the worst thing she could have done was drown her children in that flood. Children watch the way their parents work through their own loss. Their view of how Mum or Dad copes will not only affect their relationship with their parents for years to come, but it will equip them to cope with loss in their own lives. Whether it will equip them negatively or positively is up to their parents.

Many people feel they don't want to co-operate with their ex-partner at all. But if they don't, the children will suffer more than anyone else. If, for the children's sake, parents can try to work reasonably together in matters such as contact visits and child support, the children will regain a level of security and learn a way of solving problems which will stay with them for the rest of their lives.

For some couples, of course, this is impossible. If an ex-partner absolutely refuses to co-operate in any way, then the children's security is in one parent's hands alone. All that parent can do then is to try to ensure the children are not in earshot when the telephone call escalates out of control or there's a whispered exchange of abuse, and, once they're off the phone, or their ex has left, to try not to take it out on the children even though they're probably feeling furious and emotionally shaken. Above all, children shouldn't be told in graphic detail what their parent really thinks about their ex-partner's behaviour. Launching into a tirade about the other person's selfishness, hypocrisy, lack of concern and so on will do great harm to the children. An unreasonable ex-partner they may be, but they are still the children's beloved parent.

At the same time, it's important to be honest with children. While they don't need to hear one parent screaming abuse about the other, they do need to know some facts. For example, Anne's daughter kept on asking when they were going on holiday and when she'd be getting some new clothes. Anne's ex-husband wasn't paying the maintenance he should, and she was desperately short of money. Her daughter needed to know the facts – they couldn't afford a holiday or new clothes because Dad wasn't giving them as much money as he'd been asked to. She didn't explain in an abusive, angry way, which would hurt her daughter, but in a reasonable voice, so her daughter could understand the situation without being made to feel more insecure than ever.

This distinction – between being honest about the facts but not heaping every emotion on children – is very important. The children will be feeling a painful, confused sadness, and they will be questioning 'Why?' about everything that is going on. This questioning all too often takes place inside their heads, and their parents don't even realise they're asking. They don't need to hear one parent's view of the other (for their own security) but if they don't hear any facts at all, they'll panic. So if there's going to be a house move in six weeks, tell them. Don't attempt secret packing sessions when they're not looking. They'll know something is going on, and will be frightened. If you're looking for a job because you can't afford to stay at home full-time, discuss it with them. Don't start filling in application forms, or dress up and go for interviews, without letting them know what you're doing. Children are wise; they can see something

is happening, and their security will be further threatened if they're not told the truth. Don't imagine you're
protecting them from pain by not telling them.

Don't burden them with the pressure you may feel
about having to take a job or move house. Simply tell
them this is happening, and explain why it must. For
example, if you're having to find a job against your
wishes, the children will probably ask if you really want
to go out to work. It will keep them secure if they're told
some honest facts: for example, you really would like to
be at home for them, and you'd rather not have to go out
to work, but you need to earn some more money to pay
the bills. In that way, they're secure in the knowledge
that you'd like to be with them but for all your sakes you
need to finance the family. Never inflict adult problems
on them by putting it like this, even if it's how you
really feel, 'Your father is so mean and unloving that he
won't even pay to keep you, so I have to go out and earn
the money to keep you myself. It's not fair, but if I don't
do it the house will be taken away from us and we won't
even be able to afford to eat!'

So what do children really go through? What does the
bereavement journey feel like to them?

In many ways, they go through the same journey as
their parents: shock, rejection, fear, anger and guilt are
common to both the adult and the child. And yet in
other ways their pain is very different. It's easy for a parent to think, 'We're going through this together.' But
they're not. The adult has lost a partner: the child has
lost a parent. This is an entirely different experience, particularly in the case of a bitter separation, when the person who the adult sees as a bad partner is still Mummy
or Daddy to the child.

A child's thought patterns are not the same as an
adult's. The emotions the adult feels, when they think

about their partner leaving, are not usually reflected in their child's emotions. As one mother found out years later, one of her son's main worries had been, 'I am the only child in my class whose family hasn't got a car, because my daddy took it.' Focusing on such small issues, while also trying to cope with the bigger issues, can depend on their circle of friends or their school social background.

Children cope in different ways. Some withdraw, won't speak about what has happened and fall into an introverted kind of denial. Others change their behaviour in extrovert ways, sometimes showing off, becoming arrogant, violent or abusive. What is actually going on inside both types of child is the same, but in one, the anger, shock and sadness are being buried, while in the other, the emotions are being played out on the surface.

In the first shock of their loss, some children cling closely to the parent they are living with. Alongside their desperate sadness and grief, there is often a terrible fear that now one parent has gone, maybe the other one will go too. They will probably be experiencing many other anxieties about their future, such as, 'Will we still be able to live in our house? Will I still have my old friends? Will I see Daddy again now that he has gone to live so far away? Now Mummy has died who will listen to me when I want to talk about what happened at school?' Children should be given huge amounts of comforting cuddles and reassurance, and this doesn't apply only to very young children.

A child can feel angry with both his parents, not just the one who is absent. He may be furiously angry with his father, who has left, and express his fury to his mother – for instance, 'Why did you argue with him so much? He might have stayed if you'd been nicer to him!' Or if his father has died, 'Why didn't you look after him better?' If a child is able to express his anger, he should be allowed to do so. Anger is better out than in. It doesn't help a child to be told that it's wrong to be angry. It won't be pleasant for a parent to see their child in a fit of anger against his situation, but getting his anger out will help him. When the bout of anger is over, be there with comfort and a listening ear. It's a calm time for talking to each other, for the child to express how he feels and what sparked off that particular attack of anger. He needs to be reassured that his parent's love for him is unconditional, and doesn't depend on him being sweetness and light all the time.

Younger children do not have the language to express their anger, so it often comes out in behaviour. To understand a little of the powerlessness that a child feels, try to think how you would feel if you were told that you couldn't express your anger verbally, and that instead you had to draw it. What would you draw, and how would you draw it? Now relate that to a child expressing anger without words, and you may be able to see why he behaves in the way he does.

Nearly all children will feel guilty. 'It must be my fault!' is a cry common to almost every child who has lost a parent, particularly those under eleven. And it's not only found among children whose parent has chosen to leave, but also among those whose parent has been killed in an accident, or died of cancer. 'If only I had got on better with Dad; if I had been good Mummy wouldn't have left; Mummy was always telling me not to be so noisy when Daddy was ill so he must have died because I wasn't quiet enough; if I'd stopped wetting the bed Daddy wouldn't have gone.' Young children can even believe that their own thoughts made the parent disappear. A child who wished his mum would go away every night when she was telling him it was time for bed might believe that when Mum really did go away it was because he wished for it to happen. The permanent physical loss of a parent who has died can have a devastating effect on a child. Parents must make it absolutely clear to their children that whatever they did or didn't do would have made no difference. These assurances of their innocence in what happened must be repeated again and again.

Children are going to go through times of feeling unloved and rejected, despite the fact that their parent tells them they are loved. The knowledge that a parent chose to leave plays havoc with the child's self-esteem. Janet told her sons that Daddy had left because he didn't love her, not because he didn't love them. Both Daddy and Mummy still loved them, and they shouldn't doubt that. But when Daddy came to take his sons away for a few days, he brought his new lady friend with him, and the children noticed he'd taken off his wedding ring. When they returned, one of the children remarked that if their father had loved them, he wouldn't have left.

This is a common reaction. It doesn't make sense to a child to hear that a parent still loves them, but has chosen to leave them. Therefore, the child reasons, my parents must be lying when they say they love me. Nevertheless, it is incredibly important for parents to keep reassuring their children of their love for them, and to assure them that their love will continue in the future. The next question children will be asking is, 'If you can stop loving each other, perhaps you will stop loving me too.' Parents should try to explain that both Mummy and Daddy loved them from the moment they were born, and it's a love that can't change. Dad and Mum may not be husband and wife any more, but they will be Dad and Mum for the rest of their lives.

There's a temptation to start spoiling the children. Often, without the parent even realising it's happening, they try to compensate the child for the loss of the other parent. It can happen in all sorts of ways, some of them subtle, others more obvious. Life starts to revolve around the child; the parent's every decision is governed by the child's wishes. Treats that used to happen once a week are now given on demand; the children are not told off so firmly when they're defiant; they're not made to tidy up their toys, come in as early as they should or go to bed at the time they used to.

Children can be over-compensated with clothes and presents. Some single parents start buying their children 'right label' clothes, and even when they get into debt the feeling remains that they mustn't deprive them further. One mother complained bitterly to everyone regarding her poverty and debt, saying she couldn't do anything about it – but her daughter attended a private school, had private lessons out of school, designer clothes, expensive holidays and the latest computer equipment.

Parents think by doing this they're making up for something their children have lost. What they are in fact doing is making the children even less secure. Loving children means continuing to discipline them as usual. Changes in guidelines and standards will make them frightened. So much of their life is unstable at the moment, and if their parent starts moving the boundaries, what do they have to hold on to?

There's another temptation for parents: to start using their children as confidants. But a child shouldn't be an emotional prop. Sally and her ten year old daughter had a good relationship, and Sally even described them as 'close friends'. She told Laura everything – about her father's relationship with other women, his lies and inconsistencies. She even went up to Laura's room at night to fill her in on the latest details of a phone conversation she'd just had with her ex. Laura learnt of her mother's deepest emotions, her guilt and regrets. One day, Laura shouted at her mother, 'Stop telling me all these things!' and ran out of the room in tears.

However friendly a parent and child might be, this 'friend' is still a child – and the child of the ex-partner. She should not be told the details of her parent's betrayal or inadequacy. Such confidences should be saved for an adult friend or counsellor. The child has enough to cope with, as she sorts out her own unsettled emotions.

In the same way, parents shouldn't look to children to meet their own needs – the need to be significant, loved, and the need to be needed. It's a role-reversal which puts too great a burden on children, and deprives them of their own freedom.

The parent who wants to help a child through their loss should encourage communication. This means listening – and not just so that the parent can give their opinion. Children chatter at all sorts of times; often, exasperatingly, at the worst times for the parent. The most meaningful and enlightening conversations can take place when teenagers come into the kitchen late at night, even though Mum has just put the cat and the milk bottles out and is longing to get some sleep.

Children will almost certainly need some support with the contact arrangements with the other parent. How does the child view the contact arrangements? What are the repercussions of seeing the other parent? The child may be thrilled to see Dad, or Mum, but feel left out of the other family, an intruder in the new home. He may not like the new partner or step-children. There are different sets of rules in this house; he has to adapt.

Children often regard contact as stepping into another world, a little like going on holiday. If they do this, it can help them to cope better.

Parents should always be on the look-out for signs of distress, particularly after contact visits. One of Janet's sons returned home terrified of going swimming. His father had told him about how he nearly drowned when he was a child. Janet offered to take him swimming, but this was no good. Dad had undermined her, and her son felt she might let him drown. Eventually they found a male friend who could take the child swimming.

If you are the absent parent, you have to build a new and different relationship with your child. If you can't have much contact because of distance, or difficulties with your ex, keep up what contact you can. For example, send a postcard from your holiday, to say 'I'm here and I'm thinking of you.' You don't have to buy expensive presents. Sending frequent small presents, little surprises, short notes which say you care, is just as good, if not better. The child then knows they are often in your thoughts. Remember birthdays, Christmas and special commendations, perhaps when a child has done particularly well at school. Keep a journal of events in your life, so that when your children are older and may get to know you better, they can read it and fill in the gaps they've missed. Apart from anything else, keeping a journal gives you something to do, when the evenings are long and you're missing your kids.

When the children *do* visit, keep them as stable as possible. Ensure they have their own toothbrush, towel, etc., in your home, so they don't feel they're visitors. Plan carefully, and have an alternative idea in case it rains on the day you'd decided to go to the fair. Don't waste the time they're with you by criticising your ex, or your ex's new partner if they have one. They are the people your children have to live with on a regular basis, and it won't help if they're undermined all the time. Don't introduce a whole new set of rules, but try to keep to the routine and discipline they're used to at home, if that's possible. The less hassle you create, the easier the visit.

There can be great distress for children if contact visits *don't* take place. David and Simon used to wait for their mother to collect them every Sunday. Sometimes she turned up, sometimes she didn't. There was never a phone call to let them know. Their father was there to comfort and support them, and to find other exciting things to do when it became clear this was a day that Mum wasn't coming. But the distress is not always so immediate or obvious. The parent may have chosen not to have contact, or the parent the child lives with may have made it virtually impossible. In some cases, the child has been born after the break-up and yet even many years later, there remain hurt and rejection which have to be dealt with. When there's no contact because a parent has died, there is still the ongoing sense of loss and anger – the feeling that, 'other children see their parents at the weekend, why can't I?' If it's possible to have regular contact with the grandparents and relatives on the deceased parent's side, this should be encouraged.

A common fear among children who have seen bad parenting is, 'Am I going to turn out like that?', particularly as they grow up and recognise the 'weakness' of the absent parent – who may be on his fourth relationship leaving a string of children behind him, or recovering from her umpteenth alcoholic binge. After all, children do take after their parents – don't they? They can be helped to realise that they can still have hope for their own futures: that just because Mum and Dad are getting divorced, it doesn't mean they won't grow up to have a successful relationship with someone.

Fantasies that Mum and Dad will get together again are very common. They can continue after the divorce is finalised, and even after one parent has remarried. Some children think they can play a part in this reconciliation, working hard at an exam, perhaps, so that Dad will be pleased and come back. In the film *The Parent Trap*, Hayley Mills plays the parts of both twins whose parents have divorced. Even though the parents have been apart for years, live hundreds of miles from each other and one is in another relationship, the twins successfully plot to bring their parents together again. Children in the real world need to be told that this story is highly unlikely. It won't help them if one of their parents is also living in such a fantasy world, believing that their partner will return.

If a partner has died, the memory of Mum or Dad should be kept alive for the child, who should be included wherever possible, and taken to the grave or to look at their parent's name in the role book at the crematorium. It won't help them if they're not allowed to mention the parent who has died. Talk about the good times should be encouraged – the holidays, days out, activities they enjoyed together. It may appear to be upsetting to the child, but any tears shed are healing tears. At the same time, parents shouldn't try to make a saint of the parent who has died. Both parent and child will have some bad memories, and it isn't right to pretend otherwise. Children should be allowed to be angry with the parent, not only *because* they have died, but for example because they said something which hurt the child two years ago, or they never bought the new kite they'd promised. And when a child expresses such anger, he or she should not be made to feel guilty.

George, a widower with four children, believes it is very important that bereaved families have photographs

of the deceased parent in the house. A wedding photo-
graph, pictures taken on holiday with the children,
memories of happy times. But at the same time, he
warns, it is not helpful if these photographs are grouped
together and allowed to become be a shrine.

A parent shouldn't hide their own grief from the
child, neither should they ask the child to hide his.
When a parent has died, children are sometimes given
the burden of being asked to 'be strong for Mummy', or
told, 'Don't cry, Daddy would have wanted you to be
brave.' Such words have suppressed children's emotions for years, until they have come out in other, more
damaging, ways.

Other words we use need to be watched, too. Be careful how you and other people express the death of a
mother or father. They have not 'fallen asleep', they have
died and they are not coming back. However hard that
sounds, the child must know immediately that their parent has left this world and is not going to wake up. It can
be expressed gently and lovingly, but the child has to
realise the finality of his or her loss. And another reason
for not using such euphemisms: it may make the child
terrified of falling asleep at night, in case they don't
wake up either.

Those who say children 'bounce back' and 'cope well'
are usually wrong. Children have to go through the
whole bereavement experience, and even if they seem to
be coping well on the surface there will be private
storms going on inside. They should be allowed to be
happy, sad and angry, and to express their fears. And as
time goes by, children will learn to adapt, particularly if
they receive good parenting and have a strong support
system.

They can become more realistic, too. At the beginning,
they probably won't hear a word said against either of

their parents, remaining fiercely loyal if anyone dares to criticise even the parent who has hurt them. But as time goes on, they come to know and accept their parents for who they are, warts and all. Over the four years since his father left home, one boy came to realise that he wasn't going to get anywhere unless he organised things himself. His unreliable father was unable to make arrangements or plan treats, so his son did the job for him. He began to phone his dad and tell him the time and place of a football match he wanted to be taken to the next Saturday, the price of the tickets and where they could be bought. If he wanted a Christmas present, he would tell his father exactly what it was, which shop it was in and how much it cost. By taking the initiative, he knew he could at least guarantee a smattering of fathering from his weak parent, even though he had had to push for it himself.

There's no denying that children whose parents have separated feel immense pain. As one thirteen year old said, 'You can never put into words all you feel,' and an eleven year old said, 'My parents broke up nearly three years ago and I still feel hurt.' But divorce isn't always just bad news for the child. There are times when parents becoming separate can make them better parents. They're less concentrated on marital conflict and are more caring towards the children. One sixteen year old admitted, 'I was relieved by the divorce because the rows stopped.'

Single parents don't need to walk round in gloom, imagining they've wrecked their child's whole life. Scare stories abound of children from one parent families becoming delinquents and worse. But the reverse can also be true. Children who have been through a painful experience in early life often emerge as caring, loving and responsible adults. One single father of three well-adjusted and happy children said, 'I defy anyone to say my kids are doing worse than kids from a traditional family.'

Mark's story

Mark was six years old when his father left home. Until then, his life had been sheltered and safe but this changed very quickly.

'The parameters and foundations of my own world changed completely,' says Mark. 'Like most children of that age I can tell you how I felt and was affected, but I didn't see the wider picture. I became a very introverted child, so much so that my teacher at school ensured I was never left alone in case I did something foolish.

'The world kept turning, and life went on. We went to live with my maternal grandparents, and because I was so introvert I had few real friendships. Throughout my parents' divorce, I felt like a ping-pong ball although this wasn't necessarily their fault. But like many children I wanted to please both my parents – an impossible and exasperating task at times.'

Mark describes himself as an average child who went to school and had an average academic achievement. (He doesn't mention the fact that he went on to achieve a 2:1 degree.) His mother remarried when he was nearly eleven years old, which he accepted as it meant his mother would be happy and they would all be better off materially. As a teenager he says he became less egocentric and a little less introverted, but still couldn't express the pain he'd felt.

'Despite opportunities provided by my mother and others, I still kept hold of my hurt and suffering which had occurred at the time of my parents' separation and divorce. I can see that this was exasperating for people who cared for me.'

In his early twenties, Mark became engaged to Ruth. He says he will never forget what happened after Ruth met his natural father for the first time. By this time his father had left his second wife to live with another woman and her two children. As they returned home after the meeting, Ruth could see that Mark was upset. 'Then, for the first time, I actually let go,' says Mark. 'I let go of years of pain and suffering which had increased over a decade. I let go with tears and sobs, much pacing of the floor and much soul-searching.

'Looking back, I can see that life would have been much easier if I had faced up to and let go of my hurt at the time it was caused. But isn't hindsight a wonderful thing!'

Based on Mark's experiences and observations of others, he makes some suggestions and comments to help others:

- When a parent leaves home, most children will react in one of two ways. They will be extrovert, like my elder brother, who asked questions and showed emotions at the time events were unfolding; or they will be introvert, like me. I retreated, like a tortoise, into my shell, so I wouldn't be hurt any more.
- Children are often shocked, bewildered and angry, and blame themselves. They are used to taking the blame – for the noise, the mess, for being late.
- Just like all children, these youngsters need:

  Security – familiar surroundings and routine.

  Appropriate treatment – according to their age, intellect and maturity. This includes not using them as a battleground.

  Honesty – so that they have no false hopes.

  Time for sharing – about themselves. If one shares something negative, it may not seem so bad, and it will prevent it from seeming even more negative. However, sharing problems with a child as if they were an adult is not productive.

  Time together and time apart from their parents.
- When children are visiting their absent parent they will have a whole range of emotions and thoughts. Before the visit they may be anxious and excited. They need security and good planning – packing the day before, for example, may ease tension and anxiety.

During the visit the children will think of the resident parent. It may be a good idea for the resident parent to arrange to write or phone during the visit.

On the return from the visit the children will have a great need for security, so the resident parent must always be there to receive the children home.

● *A teenage girl, who did not have both parents at home, said, 'It doesn't matter if you have six parents, if they don't care. I'd rather just have one that does.' I believe that any child who thought about it could do nothing but agree with this statement. I know it's true for me.*

10

Practical ways of helping children

If you are able to give your children emotional support in the midst of your own grief and confusion, as outlined in the previous chapter, you're already doing a great job. But you probably still recognise that there are other ways in which your children need help – ways in which you need support from others.

You are the most important person to them, of course, but support from outside the home will benefit them, and will take some of the load off you at a very difficult time. Single parents shouldn't be ashamed to admit their need for help with their children. It's no longer unusual for schools, clubs or churches to hear about divorcing parents – there are an estimated 1.7 million one parent families in Britain, which is a quarter of all families. In 1998 just over 150,000 children were affected by divorce, nearly twice as many as in 1971. So people aren't going to be shocked when a friend or colleague breaks the news that they're separating or getting divorced. It's wrong for parents to think that they're protecting children by trying to keep difficult home circumstances secret from their teachers or club leaders. Quite the opposite is true: the children will be more protected once people know that one of their parents has left.

Schools can provide security for the children of a single parent family, particularly if there is a good pastoral support structure in place. Having extended family living nearby can help, if they are supportive. Youth leaders or Sunday School teachers in the local church can also make a huge difference to the children, again, if they are supportive. The 'if' has to be added – some single parents have felt condemned by their family or the church, and this adds to their pain rather than relieving it. A child can also find help from close friends of the family, as well as friends in their own peer group.

What outside help does your child need, and how can you provide it?

School

If a parent knows in advance that their partner is going to die or that they are going to separate, they should tell the school before it happens. Children will be in need of support before the event, as well as after. If the death or separation is sudden, the school should be told as soon as it's possible.

About two-thirds of children from divorced homes display marked changes in their behaviour at school. This can range from loss of concentration and daydreaming to rudeness and bullying. Teachers need to be aware of why this is happening, so they can not only understand but take steps to help. Mark's mother describes him as becoming so withdrawn after his father left that he appeared to be in a waking dream. Six year old Mark wandered round, not seeming to know where he was going. She had told his teacher what had happened at home, so the teacher was able to watch over the child closely. At one point, she even assigned another pupil to keep watch over Mark in the playground, to make sure he didn't wander out of the school grounds.

Research that has been done on the children of divorced parents shows that they do worse at school than the children of two parent families. However, it is unclear whether the cause of the problem is the divorce or the conflict between the parents before the divorce occurred. Some research has shown that the children of warring parents who go on later to divorce start to do badly at school long before the divorce occurs. This suggests it is conflict at home that is the main problem, rather than the divorce itself. Once the teacher is aware of the home situation, allowances can be made for the child, instead of a stream of bad marks and critical comments from the teacher, which merely adds to the child's pain.

In a junior school, children spend the majority of their time with one teacher; if the child is fortunate enough to have a friendly, supportive teacher, he will feel free to tell that teacher his problems if he chooses to. If the child has no such rapport with his teacher and is becoming increasingly upset at school, parents could ask the headteacher if there is another supportive adult (such as the headteacher, the school nurse or a teacher the child related to in a former class) who could provide a listening ear when the child needs it. In secondary schools, children move from classroom to classroom rather than staying with one teacher. However, there is usually a pastoral support structure in place, as well as one teacher who sees the children twice a day for registration, and a head of each year group, so a child should have at least one adult to turn to if he so chooses. In the case of pre-school children who attend playgroup or nursery, group leaders should be told about the home situation. If a previously settled child begins to cry uncontrollably for Mummy, the adults there will need to know why.

Most children don't want to be singled out for special treatment, but they do want their teachers to know. Children need as much continuation in routine as possible, and for some, school will be the only stable aspect of their lives. It's important to keep it stable for them, by keeping the staff fully informed.

Friends

A child needs to have an outlet somewhere, and he will want to tell his best friend, at least, what's going on at home. But when he puts everything into words, openly and honestly, he's going to feel disloyal. He will feel he's criticising his mum or dad, and this will provoke feelings of guilt. He needs a parent's permission to speak to his friends. Parents should tell their children that they are willing for them to speak to a close friend about private matters.

Older children often need to talk to an adult friend. It could be that there is a close friend of the family, or a Sunday School teacher, Scout or Guide leader, who is able and willing to listen to the child. It should be someone that both parent and child trust, and again, the child needs to be given his parent's permission to be as honest as he likes about his feelings.

At the same time, children shouldn't be pushed into talking to anyone. It may be that they really don't want to. Parents should go at the child's speed, simply letting them know there is someone, or a choice of people, willing and ready to listen and talk. They need to know their parent won't push them into talking to anyone until they're ready, and that it's completely up to them when the time is right, if at all. Even if they never take up the offer, at least they know they have a supportive parent who is happy for them to speak to someone, that there's someone out there for them, and that they have a choice.

Family

If you're fortunate enough to have a close family, or support from at least one or two family members, hold on to it with both hands. Children gain immense stability and a feeling of continuity from a good relationship with a friendly aunt or a beloved grandad. It may be that the listening ear mentioned above will be found within the family, and the child will have no need of anyone outside. If Grandad or Auntie don't live locally, let your child phone them whenever they like (despite the cost), and go and stay with them for holidays, sometimes on their own if possible.

If the supportive family happen to be in-laws, there can be complications. Single parents who have always felt close to their in-laws can find as good a support system there as within their own family. If, however, the in-laws prove to be on the side of their son or daughter who has left the family home, you may feel alienated from them, and yet they are still your child's grandparents, aunts, uncles, cousins. If the grandad that your child loves so much is the father of your ex, you may have a personal struggle in allowing them to spend time together. However you feel, the child must come first – it's going to cause him even more confusion if you attempt to put up barriers between them. If your child has a good relationship with a close family member, don't stand in their way, even if you have problems with that person. Your animosity towards your ex should not extend to their parents or wider family.

Grandads can be the next best thing to dads. If Dad is the absent parent, then grandfathers have an important role to play in the single parent household, if they are allowed to do so. Boys in particular need a male role model, and girls will appreciate the fatherly discipline. It's hard for a single mum to be both mother and father to a child, so be grateful if there's a grandad who can provide a stable father-substitute.

Role models

The most important role models for children are their parents, and parents shouldn't underestimate this. Although accepting this fact may put extra stress on you, the truth is that your child will be watching your reactions, methods of coping and ability to overcome circumstances. Parents who are struggling with all this should get help for themselves. It will in the long run help their child too.

You may be fortunate enough to have an ex-partner who provides a good role model to your children. If your ex is still being a good father or mother, try to co-operate as much as you can. Ensure adequate contact with the children.

However, it's estimated that two-thirds of fathers never see their children again within two years of divorce. Other absent parents may still see their children, but may for some reason not offer an adequate father- or mother-figure. Some children may have lost a parent through death. So when a motherless daughter approaches adolescence, or a fatherless son appears to have no concept of masculinity, how can they be supported?

The importance of having close family and friend is not only to supply love, friendship, security and a listening ear, but also to provide role models to your children. If there doesn't seem to be anyone among your friends or family to fulfil that role, take another look around.

It could be that the father of your son's best friends is already providing a role model, albeit unconsciously. Could you talk to both parents, admitting your son's need for a father-figure? They might offer to take your son with them to the next football match they're attending, or on a fishing trip, or even on holiday. Even just having him round regularly for tea could make a difference to his view of fathers.

In the same way, a father bringing up a daughter alone could talk to the parents of her best friend. Perhaps the friend's mother could take your child along when she next goes shopping with her own daughter for clothes – with you providing the money for your daughter, of course. She might even include your daughter in conversations about puberty, menstruation, teenage years – all those things that a father might feel unable to discuss. It's unlikely another parent would want to intrude on such matters, unless you actually admit you're in need of such help.

Likewise, Sunday School teachers, Guide or Scout leaders might be making attempts to befriend your child, but won't know how far you'd like them to take the friendship. Find out if your child feels an affinity with any of his club leaders, then let the leader know that your child might find it helpful to speak to them in more depth, and ask them if they'd be willing to look for further opportunities to help.

Normal life
A child's whole life may be overtaken by their home circumstances, and they may not be able to function in their usual pursuits. But it's important for their well-being that they carry on with their customary activities.

If, before her dad died or her mum left home, your daughter attended piano lessons on Monday afternoons, Guides on Thursday evenings and drama club on Saturday mornings, encourage her to continue. Don't push her too hard in the early days; she won't see the point in practising for her grade three piano exam the day after her mum's funeral. But she should gradually pick up the pieces of her social life in the weeks following the death or separation. Carrying on out-of-school activities will encourage her to look beyond her own problems and grief, will help her keep her own identity and will boost her self-worth. If nothing else, they will provide a diversion.

Your children need you, other caring and supportive adults and their own friends, and they need their normal life to continue. The end of a relationship does not have to mean the end of all their other relationships. The loss of the way of life they knew doesn't mean life is over. Find practical support for your children's sake, and for your own.

Victoria's story

Victoria wasn't even born when her parents split up. Her mother was three months pregnant, and had two young sons, at the time her father left to live with another woman.

When Victoria was six weeks old, her father came to the house, looked in the carrycot, then walked away. The performance was repeated when she was two. As a court appearance was due and her father wanted to be seen as a responsible parent, he came to visit her again. He entered the room, looked at the toddler, then left.

Now fifteen, and having spent most of her life with another dad – her mother's second husband – Victoria is still more affected by the events that happened before her birth than many people realise. 'I feel rejected that my dad doesn't want to know me or have anything to do with me,' she says. 'I feel there's something missing. I'm ashamed when I tell my friends that my real dad doesn't want to know me now, and isn't interested in me. Because of this I feel there's something wrong with me, and that no one likes me or cares for me. I feel jealous of other children having and knowing their real dad.'

Victoria's father is now on his third marriage, having left his second wife in the same way he left his first.

Victoria is indignant on her brothers' behalf. 'Doesn't he care about my brothers? He left them and he hurt them. How can he do it? Can anyone trust him, or believe what he says?' she asks.

Based on her experience of being the child of a single parent, Victoria has drawn up a list of do's and don'ts, to help people care for other children in similar positions.

- *DON'T say you know what it's like if you've not been there yourself.*
- *DON'T tell them everything is OK.*
- *DON'T let them down, because they've already been let down by their parent.*

- ● *DO tell them they're not the only one, and they're not on their own.*
- ● *DO tell them they can phone or come to see you or write a letter whenever they feel it's necessary.*
- ● *DO suggest they meet with other children in similar situations – teenagers will usually want to meet with other teenagers. They might also want to talk with an adult who went through a similar experience as a child, but who has come through and may now be happily married.*
- ● *DO give them a hug and make them feel special and wanted. Tell them you love them, but more importantly, God loves them. He's always there, no matter what happens or what they do, he's still there for them and he loves them as a dad.*

11

Onward and upward

When the children leave home, and single parents find themselves on their own, they are faced with a whole new set of circumstances. As Jennifer told us (see chapter 5), she was having to adapt from 'single parent' to 'single person' now her children had grown up and left home, and it wasn't easy. Angela told us she was at first bereft when her youngest child went to college; she said there was an inevitable gap, but it grew easier as time passed. So is there anything single parents can do to prepare themselves for those years?

Being prepared is all-important, for the children as much as the parent. The children need to be prepared to cope alone when they leave home, and not to feel responsible for their parent. There's a kind of role reversal that can take place once a child reaches adulthood and realises that when he goes, he'll be leaving Mum or Dad all alone. But the responsibility for the parent is not theirs.

Even though Mum or Dad may long to cling on to their offspring for as long as possible, they have to let them go for the children's own sake. It's wonderful if teenagers have learnt to care for their parents but they should be helped to find the balance between care for their parents and responsibility for them. After all, parents have brought their children up to be independent. Now the children have to go out and exercise that independence, without spending their whole time worrying about the parent they've left behind.

The relationship has changed. No longer are you the parent who meets all the children's needs, but a companion for your children when they come to visit you. They shouldn't have to listen to you constantly complaining, 'Why don't you phone more often?'

One of the ways you can help them to stop worrying is to show them you're coping fine without them. For those single parents who enjoy a fulfilling career, huge interests and a busy social life, there may be little problem here. Parents sometimes relish the complete freedom they have now the house is their own and they are free to pursue their chosen activities without having to make meals or provide a taxi service for their teenagers. For others, though, their children have been the be-all and end-all of existence. Once the children have left, life becomes aimless. It's easy for this emptiness to turn into severe depression, and a new reason for living needs to be found quickly. It is much less painful if parents see this situation coming, and find new interests, friendships, jobs, etc., in advance of their children's departure.

A new way of life won't immediately happen; it has to be looked for and worked at. You may think, 'Not again!' You've been through all this before, when your husband or wife died or left home. You struggled to create a new life without your partner; now you've got to start all over again, adapting to life without the children.

It doesn't help that, as you're only too aware, you're getting older. You're coping with your ageing self at the same time as your relationship with your teenagers is changing. For women, the mood swings and complications of the menopause can cause even more despair, while men might be struggling with the midlife crisis, wondering who they are, and if any woman would still find them attractive. Eyesight gets noticeably worse; hair is greying rapidly; waistlines thicken; lines make grooves in the face. It can't be avoided – it happens to everyone. But to a single parent whose children are leaving home, facing a lonely, ageing future can be very depressing.

But life doesn't end at fifty or fifty-five, any more than it ends at forty. Grey hair or no grey hair, there can still be a great future ahead.

Melanie's husband had committed suicide when her son and daughter were teenagers. Three years later, her son was married but she still had her daughter Alison at home. After a few more years, when Alison was preparing for her own wedding, Melanie started to have panic attacks. These continued after the wedding, when, for the first time in many years, Melanie lived alone. She began to take sleeping pills every evening, to get her through the long nights. She knew she had a choice – to go under, or to make a fulfilling life for herself. She chose the latter. She realised women of her age were by no means 'past their sell-by date' and she picked herself up, continued with her job, made new friends, found many social commitments and soon started to find life hectic, although she still found time to enjoy her grandchildren.

Kathryn planned her future well in advance of the children leaving home. She was going to enrol at university as a mature student and study for a degree, and at the weekends she would do some voluntary work. She also prepared mentally for the feelings she knew she was going to have, and determined to be joyful for the things she had instead of grieving for what she'd lost. She listed the things she said she'd always wanted to do during those tied years when her children were very young, and saw the future as the opportunity for doing them. She also decided to see wrinkles and grey hairs as something to be proud of, a kind of medal for years of service.

As for that theory that you're now a 'single person' and no longer a 'single parent', think again about that. Once a parent, always a parent. The children may have left but they're not lost forever. Whether they're students (who often seem to come back to use the washing machine if nothing else!) or married and coming to visit you with their own family, they're still your children, and always will be.

Geoff's story

In 1982, Geoff's wife left home, claiming that the marriage had been a mistake on her part. His daughter, Alice, was six years old.

He has described his initial feelings as desolation, devastation and depression. How would he manage to run a home, bring up Alice and keep a full-time job? Then, after six months' separation, his wife returned, and he was overjoyed. But his joy was short lived. A week later, she left again, this time for good. It took twelve months for Geoff to accept the reality of the situation. He and Alice were going to be on their own.

Geoff's employers were understanding, and allowed him to work during school hours. Without that, he feels he would have had to give up his job. But he found little such sympathy from his church, although he did receive help from individual Christian friends, which he feels compensated for the lack of church support. One older couple he had known for years became like a new set of parents. 'They decided to adopt me,' says Geoff.

He was also helped by contact with other single parents. Initially, this was through letter-writing. 'I discovered that it was therapeutic just being able to write,' he says. 'It also made me aware that others were going through similar experiences. Indeed, many were suffering so much more than I was, and it helped me to keep my own difficulties in perspective.'

Although Geoff's family lived at the other side of the country, his mother visited during school holidays to help out, and he relied on friends to babysit when necessary. But he felt limited in the time he could be away from the home.

Geoff says he now describes himself as 'domesticated', but he knows that a mother would have had more understanding of a daughter going through the teenage years. He gave Alice literature to read as she approached puberty, but couldn't cope with speaking to her about such personal matters.

'Alice was always closer to me than to her mum, so in some ways it didn't seem to make too much difference to her when her mum left. But I'm sure she has been affected by a lack of maternal love and care – although she was quite close to my own mother, who frequently came to stay with us.'

Now that Alice is older, Geoff knows he has to make his own life as well, and admits he has got into a bit of a rut. He fears remarriage, in case a similar thing happened again. But he also fears being on his own for the rest of his life. He says one of the worst things that was said to him was that scripturally the circumstances of the divorce would make it impossible for him to remarry.

He still finds loneliness is his greatest problem, and has tried to deal with it by getting out of the house, becoming more involved in the church, walking or visiting friends. He feels particularly lonely at weekends and at New Year.

'Much time has passed since the beginning of my journey of single parenthood,' Geoff continues. 'We are still on our own but Alice has reached the age of independence, has a job and does her own thing! I no longer feel that I am a single parent, but I do have a real sympathy for other single parents. Alice still visits her mum on a regular basis and I'm glad there is a normal but limited relationship between them.

'In the early days, there was a lot of pain and sadness. But I can honestly say that, through God's grace and in God's time, so much of the hurt has been erased from my mind, and I have no bitterness over what has happened.'

12

Positive as one

Have you ever thought about single parenting as an exciting opportunity – a challenge, a chance to grow? If it's all seemed painful so far, have you considered trying to turn this pain into something positive?

Single parenthood may be a situation you have not chosen. You may be an unmarried mother who wanted to be married; a widow or widower who didn't want your partner to die; a separated or divorced parent who wishes it was otherwise. But faced with the fact that you are a single parent, you can find there are compensations.

You now have the opportunity to discover yourself, the real you. Coming to terms with the pains and effects of the past and facing the challenge of discovering who you really are can be frightening yet exciting. After experiencing pain, you can find great pleasure and joy in the little things of life; you can discover what's really important to you, and learn to value your children, your health and your friendships.

Many single parents develop a very close relationship with their children. You can have great pride in their achievements, large and small, because you know the pain they've been through. When Christine's son won an award only nine months after his father left, she was thrilled. It gave her encouragement that her son had developed and matured through such a difficult time. And some years later, when her other son was presented with his honours degree, she says she must have been the proudest parent in the cathedral. 'Only he and I knew that he had been so affected by all that had happened that he had "stood still" educationally for years and had needed extra help in his primary school,' she says.

While you take pride in their achievements, you can also be proud of yourself. Many single parents know the feeling, 'That's my son up there! I brought him up, and now look at him!' This might also be the time to feel a sense of personal achievement by taking up a different career, a course of study or a fulfilling new hobby.

There may be less tension in the parent-child relationship. You can make decisions yourself, and you don't have to disagree with someone else about what your child can or can't do. Children can't play one against the other, or be confused by two different directives. When Mum says no, the child can't run to Dad to try and get his or her own way. The parent the child lives with will be the main authority and set the standards acceptable in the family unit.

Look at the positives for your children, too. Instead of living in gloom and guilt over the damage that you think may have been done to them, look instead at the way they've learnt to be more independent. They may become more sensitive to other hurting children and, as they grow, to other adults. Experiencing pain and difficulty is necessary to their development. You spend so much time trying to protect them from such hurt, but if children are totally protected from the hard side of life they will find it much more difficult to cope as adults. Michael was so cushioned from conflict, coming as he did from a close-knit family where there was hardly ever a cross word, that when he married he didn't know how to cope with arguments. The first time he and his wife argued, he thought divorce was round the corner. It took years for him to get used to quarrels as a way of clearing the air, to be followed by apologies and forgiveness and life continuing as usual. He found that friends whose parents had split up were much more able to deal with conflict in their own relationships than he was.

You can become more confident and competent in ways you never imagined. A single mum finds she can tackle the decorating; a single dad discovers he can make his child's birthday cake. Christine was given an old, battered Mini soon after her husband left home. There was one problem. She was terrified of driving it! She'd held a driving licence for years, but seldom drove the car – her husband saw to that! Suddenly, she was to be the sole driver, and responsible for three young lives. A frightening thought at the time, yet now she drives all over the country, and even through London.

You have freedom from another person. It may not be your choice, and you may want to give it up for another relationship, but now you have it, you can use it. You have the independence to organise the day without reference to another adult, or to go away for the weekend considering only the children. How you use your time and resources is your decision. One newly-single mother went out and bought a colour TV (her husband wouldn't let the family have one); another was able to socialise and build new friendships; yet another had her ears pierced.

There's no doubt that being a single parent can be a fulfilling and satisfying experience if you allow it to be.

Let some single parents finish the book by speaking for themselves.

'There's only one set of rules at home. I get to make all the choices. When we moved I chose the house and the place – it made me feel confident and good. I've learnt that I can cope with almost anything practically. I've discovered what I like doing – things I'd not realised before, like birdwatching, rambling and reading.'

'I have a closer relationship with the children now. I can give more time to them now I don't have to give time to my husband. I love my independence and autonomy, not having to answer to anyone, making my own decisions, being in control of the finances.'

'I have a second chance at being a child. I can see Christmas like a child again – and no one to criticise me!'

'I have no one to boss me or nag me. I can cook what I like and when I want. I have a little bit of independence. I've learnt you don't have to have a husband to be a family. I've learnt that I can cope, that I can do things myself – sometimes better than people who have a partner. I've learnt to be more assertive, that I'm not a failure and that I'm as good as other people. I've learnt to be me.'

'I've found peace, the joy of new friends, less tension, no depression, much better health – and I'm braver. I have so much self-assurance now. I've discovered that you can enjoy fruit-picking, very cheap holidays and car boot sales.'

'I have come more and more to find myself and to be myself. I'm stronger than I thought and I'm capable of more than I thought. We communicate well as a family and face many issues of real life together. I'm loved and valued by many people and by God.'

Addresses of Support Organisations

Cruse Bereavement Care
126 Sheen Road
Richmond
Surrey TW9 1UR
Tel: 020 8939 9530
Support for anyone who has been bereaved.

Gingerbread Association for One Parent Families
7 Sovereign Court
London E1W 3HW
Tel: 020 7488 9300
website: www.gingerbread.org.uk
email: generalenquiry@gingerbread.org.uk
Support, social events and an advice line.

National Association of Child Contact Centres
Minerva House
Spaniel Road
Nottingham
NG1 6EP
Tel: 0115 948 4557
website: www.naccc.org.uk
email: naccc.org.uk
A nationwide network of contact centres which provide a neutral venue for contact when there is no viable alternative.

National Council for One Parent Families
255 Kentish Town Road
London NW5 2LX
Helpline: 0800 185026
website: www.oneparentfamilies.org.uk
email: info@oneparentfamilies.org.uk
A wide range of information on benefits, tax, legal rights, child support, returning to work, etc.

Parentline Plus
520 Highgate Studios
53–79 Highgate Road
London
NW5 1TL
Tel: 020 7284 5500
Freephone helpline: 0808 800 2222
website: www.parentlineplus.org.uk
A telephone helpline for parents and step-parents under stress.

Christian Organisations

Care for the Family
PO Box 488
Cardiff CF15 7YY
029 2081 0800
website: www.careforthefamily.org.uk
email: mail@cff.org.uk
Resources and events to encourage parents and strengthen family life. Includes a regular newsletter for single parents, links with others and holidays.

Child Link (Care)
Challenge House
29 Canal Street

Glasgow
G4 0AD
Low-cost number: 0845 6011134
email: cs@care.org.uk
A referral helpline on child care issues.

Credit Action
6 Regent Terrace
Cambridge
CB2 1AA
Freephone helpline: 0900 591084
website: www.creditaction.com
email: credit.action@dial.pipex.com
Free financial advice, especially on getting out of debt.

Mothers' Union
24 Tufton Street
London
SW1P 3RB
Tel: 020 7222 5533
website: www.themothersunion.org
email: mu@themothersunion.org
Offers 'Away from it all' holidays for families under stress who cannot afford a holiday.

PCCA Christian Child Care
PO Box 133
Swanley
Kent
BR8 7UQ
Low-cost number: 0845 1204550
website: www.pcca.co.uk
email: info@pcca.co.uk
Advice for those concerned about child abuse.

Single Parent Network
c/o Care for the Family
Address as above
An association that supports and encourages individuals and groups working with and for those who, for whatever reason, parent alone. A directory of national and local initiatives.

The Association of Christian Counsellors
173a Wokingham Road
Reading
Berkshire
RG6 1LT
Tel: 0118 9662207
website: www.doveuk.com/acc
email: office@acc-uk.org
Supplies details of Christian counsellors around the UK.

Further reading

Alexander, Helen, *Experiences of Bereavement* (Lion, 1997)

Beardshaw, Tom, Guy Hordern, Christine Tufnell, *Single Parents in Focus* (Care for the Family, 2000)

Castle, Fiona, *Rainbows Through The Rain* (Hodder & Stoughton, 1998)

Compston, Christopher, *Breaking Up Without Cracking Up* (HarperCollins, 1998)

Francis, Paul, *Teenagers: The Parent's One Hour Survival Guide* (HarperCollins, 1998)

Hepden, Steve, *Explaining Rejection* (Sovereign World, 1996)

Parsons, Rob, *The Sixty Minute Father* (Hodder & Stoughton, 1995)

Parsons, Rob, *The Sixty Minute Mother* (Hodder & Stoughton, 2000)

Smoke, Jim, *Single Again* (Servant Publications, 1999)

Wilkinson, Helena, *Breaking Free From Loneliness* (Marshall Pickering, 1997)

Books for Children

Ironside, Virginia, *The Huge Bag Of Worries* (Macdonald Young Books, 1996)

Jordan, Diane Louise, *Why Are My Parents Separating?* (Story tapes with parental booklet) (Backbone Productions Ltd, PO Box 28409, London N19 4WX)

Stern, Zoe & Evan, *Divorce Is Not the End of the World* (Zoe's and Evan's Coping Guide for Kids) (Tricycle Press, 1997)